REDEFINING THE CORPORATE SOUL

REDEFINING THE CORPORATE SOUL

HOW TO BUILD A CORPORATE SOUL AND CREATE A SUCCESSFUL BUSINESS

BY

KURT GASSNER

Redefining The Corporate Soul
Kurt Gassner

Impressum
My-mindguide – The publishing trademarke of trendguide Capital GmbH, Klenzestr. 42a, 80469 Munich, Germany.

Reg. Nr. HRB Munich 206639, VAT 152 123 159, CEO: Kurt Friedrich Gassner
Web: www.my-mindguide.com, mail: gassner@my-mindguide.com

Paperback ISBN: 978-3-98793-916-7
Hardback ISBN: 978-3-98793-036-2

TABLE OF CONTENTS

WELCOME

It's connected to your own spirit, but it's distinct from you in every way. Even though you and your creative calling created it, it possesses its own innate life force, sense of direction, and destiny. To expand and express itself following its actual essence, like all souls, it has an inherent drive. Taking advantage of this unique opportunity, you can establish a close relationship with the Soul of Your Business and accept its inherent sovereignty while aligning it with your soul. Your business and personal life will flourish then result.

Your company has the potential to develop into what it was always meant to be. In addition to financial success, it can help you in various other ways. It's a great place for you to grow and evolve. As a site from which your love radiates most strongly into the world, it can be transformed. It's a fact that many entrepreneurs are unaware of. You regard your business as a thing to which strategies and tactics must be applied for it to operate as a proper business and consistently produce money. It's a gradual surrender of your power to numerous marketing experts who are eager to advise you on the "proven" approach to grow your company. You resort to controlling your business in order to achieve the desired success, based on what experts have informed you is required.

It's easy to feel like a tyrant when you're trying to fit the radiance of your vocation into the newest recipe for company success so you can earn the money you need and join the ranks of all those happy testimonial people. There is a tendency to believe that a business must look a specific way to succeed even though the inherent intelligence in your business requires something entirely different. However, you are blissfully ignorant of this fact. How did you do that? This isn't being discussed in the business community. When you set out to accomplish your great work, the excitement you felt at the beginning turns to frustration. When you doubt your ability to make a living doing what you truly love, it can be hard to get back on your feet. You could get locked in a thriving but old form of your business and not be able to hear how it wants to evolve into a newer, truer representation. Fortunately, there is an alternative. Forgetting that your company is an extension of yourself creates the opportunity to develop an emotional connection. This allows you to ask the Soul of Your Business what it needs in order to be honest and how you can support that. Read on to find out more.

Corporate soul

INTRODUCTION

Every business has a soul. There is a unique set of values for every business that shapes its priorities and conduct. What does it mean when someone says, "You've got a lot of soul" or "You're an old soul"? Humans can gain a sense of a person's essence even though they can't see or touch their literal soul. If your clients have a lasting impression of your brand after having used your product, service, or team, then you've achieved success. Even if no one has ever said it, you should strive to make your customers feel as if your company has a tremendous soul.

Customers remember purposeful brands in today's world. Brands with a strong sense of purpose are more likely to have satisfied customers, a happier workforce, and a larger market share. If you want your business to have a personality, giving it a distinct purpose is essential. Clients learn what your company's goals are, how it plans to address its issues, and why it was founded in the first place. An organization's impact and results will increase if it has a clear mission and aims to improve the communities in which it operates.

As long as businesses break their commitments and betray trust, the people will be outraged by their carelessness. Despite this, most people have little choice but to work or invest in corporations. On the job, how can we balance our cynicism with our desire for meaning and trust in the workplace? How can we tell if our company is headed in the right direction, not only financially but in all other aspects? Are you a corporation with a heart and soul? You're in good company. There is yet hope. Executives, managers, employees, and entrepreneurs looking for guidance on spotting problem areas and bringing attention to harmful practices will find it in this clear, hard-hitting guide. Also, for those concerned about the work they do and the principles they uphold, there is a lot to learn in this great psychological corporate book.

I've worked for 40 years in brand consulting and brand advertising. Towards the end, I worked as a brand auditor to measure the core brand values of worldwide operating companies. Therefore I traveled the world and interviewed all stakeholders of a brand: Employers, Clients, Collaborators. I learned the importance of a company's soul and how important it is to live up to these values. "Body-Soul-Spirit" is one not only with us humans but also in the world of companies. So – if you choose a new workplace or a company where you want to spend your valuable lifetime – check first if the SOUL of the company is a soul match for you. Does the company live up to their soul, or is it only written on a glossy piece of paper?

CHAPTER I

ASK YOUR SUBCONSCIOUS FIRST – DIVE DEEP AND EXPLORE YOUR INNER THOUGHTS

Your subconscious mind can provide solutions to any issues you face. Everyone has access to this amazing and effective asset, but realizing its full potential requires that you grasp its full scope and scope of application. Because your subconscious mind receives hundreds of ideas and beliefs every day, it must be able to distinguish between the most significant ones and those that don't matter. The solutions to your queries and clarifications will appear in the most amazing way. When it comes down to it, we have nothing but our own experiences to rely on. A person's entire existence can be based on the belief that experiencing or going through a specific event or incident will provide them with long-term joy. Consciously seeking relief from discomfort, we naturally gravitate away from it toward pleasure. This is the fundamental definition of unconsciousness. To find a purpose in life may be to raise children or develop a great business focused on our core principles, or sometimes it may just be to enjoy a new relationship, new automobile, or beautiful vacation. Searching for ultimate spirituality could also be the motivation.

There are times in life when you feel like everything is coming apart and you're not sure what to do next. Now is the moment to go deep within yourself because you already have all the answers you're looking for. The greatest way to really get to know yourself is to let go of everything and spend a few minutes just focusing on yourself. One of the best ways to learn about yourself spiritually is to do it this way.

Ask yourself, "What will/does it give me?" if you're thinking about what you want in life. If you keep asking yourself that, eventually, you'll uncover your deepest desire: the sensation you long for. It's common for people to discover that what they're looking for in a new relationship is an inner sense of connection or excitement they believe they can't get in the here and now. We're all on the lookout for new experiences, and we tend to think that they may be found in the everyday things around us. Humans, objects, and substances. It's true that when we find what we're looking for, it's a nice feeling of accomplishment. After the honeymoon period is over and the holiday hysteria subsides, we tend to crave those states once more (and often in addictive ways).

During hypnosis, our bodies begin reproducing whatever we experience in our subconscious mind or unconscious,'" as if it were real. Often in hypnosis, people might begin to experience great states of liberation, joy, and unity in ways they can only fathom. When you go on 'inner-mind travels,' you discover that your mind follows you wherever you go. A personal relationship with one's thoughts and inner world helps one's mind transform into something meaningful, something that sticks with one and alters one's perspective on what is possible. Through active participation, you can begin to develop a relationship with your truest self, allowing you to move beyond the realm of the just physical.

Most people use their subconscious minds to solve their difficulties and obstacles. There are only two options: either give up trying to find a solution or ask for input from those with less knowledge and experience than ourselves. Anyone in poverty would never give you advice on how to become a millionaire, but we heed the advice of those who lack what we seek. Whenever you accept and believe in your subconscious mind, it will invariably supply the solutions. To find an answer, you must be patient and recognize that your subconscious can solve the issue. Asking and receiving answers to all of your inquiries can be easier with the following information.

HOW TO ASK YOUR SUBCONSCIOUS MIND QUESTIONS

Put Your Thoughts Down On Paper. Every day, your brain is bombarded with more than 80,000 new ideas, emotions, and desires. Your subconscious mind may have difficulty sorting through them and finding what's most important to you. When you're bombarded with the same thoughts over and over, they begin to shape your reality. It's critical that you put all of your attention on the things you truly desire because, if you don't, they'll appear as undesired objects. When you're looking for an answer to a problem or a query, your subconscious mind is the only place to turn. Avoid rushing to find answers and instead take your time thinking through the issues at hand.

Time is needed to search through the billions of memories you have stored in your subconscious mind. As a result of this ability, the subconscious mind may tap into infinite knowledge and wisdom, allowing it access to information that is otherwise unavailable. Do it again if you don't get an answer within 12 hours. When you ask the same question repeatedly, your subconscious knows that the answer is important to you. Recall that your subconscious mind receives millions of queries each year, which gets overwhelmed by the volume. Concentrate on a single issue at a time to reduce the complexity of your request.

Before You Go To Sleep, Present the Issue. There is no such thing as a 'sleep cycle' for your subconscious mind, and you can take advantage of this. Compose your written statement or query on paper before going to bed at night. Hand the question to your subconscious mind once you've drafted it. When you go to sleep, your subconscious mind gets to work on your request. It has access to all of your stored knowledge, which could be in the billions or trillions of bytes. When faced with a difficult situation, you have the power to ask and find a solution. Believing that your subconscious mind contains the answers to your questions is essential if you want to reach your full potential.

To access your subconscious mind's wisdom, you must be clear and specific in your request.' If you ask a question that's too broad, you'll get answers that aren't clear. Therefore, be specific in your question, and your subconscious mind will assist you in discovering the answer. To improve your chances of success and to ensure that your subconscious mind understands exactly what you're asking, be as specific as possible in your writing. In your description of your problem, be as thorough as possible, delving deep into the issue's root causes. It's in the details where mastery is found, and your subconscious mind will take note of your desire and begin brainstorming solutions. Asking my subconscious for money-making suggestions is an example of a vague query. A simple plea for money won't accomplish anything if it isn't followed up with a detailed explanation of why that money is so important to me. The subconscious will begin to draw in ideas and thoughts to make it a reality.

Spend Some Time Alone To Ponder Things. When you've answered your question and given your subconscious mind a full synopsis, it's time to open the subconscious mind and let it solve the issue. Meditation, soothing music, or binaural beats can all help you relax for 10 minutes at a time. The goal is to cultivate a theta brain wave, which allows your subconscious mind to be exposed to the ideas. To solve an issue, you must first silence your analytical mind (your conscious mind). You can't solve the problem since the conscious mind doesn't know the answer. The analytical part of your brain should be turned off so that when you enter the theta brain state, that part of your brain is no longer active. Then your brain goes into a trance, and your subconscious mind takes over.

Use Gratitude And Thankfulness As A Way To Boost Your Mood. Allow yourself a moment of thankfulness and thanksgiving before going to bed. The more you practice gratitude, the more positive your ideas and outlook become. Gratefulness is contagious, bringing additional good vibes and admiration. Allowing the subconscious mind to open itself up to new possibilities is what you are doing. What are the things in your life that you're grateful for? How many of those things can you name? Then, praise your subconscious mind for finding the answers by expressing gratitude. It's more likely that your subconscious mind will pick up on what you're saying and deliver an answer more quickly. Everyone, including our subconscious mind, enjoys receiving compliments.

Use headphones to listen to a positive affirmation throughout the night. Insomnia has no place in the subconscious. As a result, these are the best times to use affirmations or hypnosis to work on your subconscious mind. When pondering a query for the subconscious, use affirmations that reflect that question in spirit. There are many other ways to increase your wealth, such as listening to positive statements about money. You can use affirmations to change your state of mind so. An affirmation can assist you with a wide range of issues. If that fails, you can record a statement or a combination of statements that will help you get the responses you want and then use that as the basis for your own affirmation.

HOW TO TAP INTO YOUR SUBCONSCIOUSNESS

There are many ways to access your higher self and go to the base of your soul other than meditating and praying. All of us have access to an extensive reservoir of wisdom, information, and intellect in our subconscious minds. A person's destiny can be altered by mastering the subconscious mind's ability. Having a lot of things is easy, whether it's money, things you own, success in your career or personal relationships, good health, or general well-being.

Work on your Soul Traveling skills. Getting to know yourself on a deeper level through the practice of "soul wandering" is becoming increasingly popular. Using this method is the finest technique for you to delve deep within yourself, and it's also employed by a lot of spiritual trainers and experts. As a means of liberating your soul, soul travel allows you to connect with the other world already within you. Doing this can help you become more self-aware in all parts of your life.

Here are a few measures you should do to travel to your higher self and dive deep into your soul to assist you better understand: You must first choose a place where you can sit in peace and ensure that there are no distractions; then you must enter into a deep meditation state and relax your mind. Let go of all the thoughts and sensations you've been experiencing throughout the day. Assume that you can ascend further into the cosmos and simply float toward the central sun. Stay as long as you like and ask your soul whatever questions you may have about your own life. To get your body to move your fingers again, you must tell it what to do. You might also express gratitude and appreciation for the opportunity to meet and converse with your own soul. Lay there and begin to move slowly as you recall all you've felt and seen. To begin with, you need to be careful because this is a really profound practice, and your spirit may not want to return. That's why it's a good idea to have a friend on standby who can assist you in regaining consciousness of your body.

Find What You're Passionate About. In order to get a better sense of who you are, you should do this first. There are many people who go about their day-to-day lives without ever figuring out what they truly desire. Having a happy existence is something that most people take for granted. Many believe that money is the key when it comes to discovering oneself. While this may be true for some, it defies logic to assert that wealth can bring happiness to everyone. So finding out what really matters to you is essential so that you may deep dive into yourself and do the things that identify you and make you happy. You should evaluate your day and see how many things you do for yourself that you truly care about. What you'll be amazed to learn is that the vast majority of people simply go about their daily routines without a purpose in mind. You need to start doing things that will allow you to better understand your thoughts and find your true self.

When you meditate, your creative juices flow, and your ambition is fulfilled. In this way, it aids in integrating your conscious and subconscious thoughts, allowing you to access the potential of your unconscious mind. It helps you stay in the here and now, which is essential for connecting with your subconscious mind. Get into the habit of meditating each and every day. Make sure you're in an area where you won't be disturbed. Check to see that your body is in a relaxed position before continuing. Utilize a meditation tool, such as a visual image, music, or mantra to help you focus and silence your mind. This skill can be learned, but it will require time and effort. Distracting thoughts should be carefully released, and your mind brought back to your chosen focus method whenever your mind starts to wander. As your mental state improves, you'll notice a reduction in the amount of noise you're hearing. Meditating gets easier with practice. When you've reached a state of complete relaxation and stillness, focus your thoughts on your goals and dreams. Your subconscious mind will be influenced by what you focus on at this moment. At a certain frequency, you'll begin to attract things of the same frequency.

Invest Time In What You Are Passionate About. As you may be aware, most people are unable to pursue their true passion for a variety of reasons. To get to know yourself, you'll have to accomplish something that you're truly passionate about. In order to get to know yourself better, this is the only way to focus all of your attention on one item. Don't worry about quitting your career just yet; take some time to indulge in your passions. Isolating yourself from the rest of the world for a while will help you work more efficiently.

Keep your mind always focused on the present moment. You must have a clear vision of what you want to achieve in life. Do not worry about how you'll do it; all you need to do is develop a clear and compelling vision. Visualizing things can help you to achieve them. To achieve your goals, you must have faith in your abilities. Know it is possible. Doubt and pessimism will only hinder your aspirations, goals, and desires. Some people make a list of their goals. In certain cases, people keep a scrapbook to record their dreams and aspirations. In this way, you can keep your goals in perspective and feel like they're within your grasp. Affirmations can help you stay focused on your goals.

You should pay attention to your intuition and act on it when necessary. Consciousness receives these messages from the subconscious. It's not a good idea to give things a deadline. Allow things to happen at their own pace instead of worrying about them. Remove time constraints from activities by focusing on the present moment. In contrast to the conscious mind, which is constantly curious, doubtful, and disbelieving, the subconscious mind makes no such inquiries. Because of this, it accepts everything it is told as gospel. Try to cultivate pleasant, loving, harmonious, and positive thoughts in your mind so that your subconscious mind can support these thoughts.

Develop the habit of just speaking to yourself with positive and constructive thoughts. Things that you think about are constantly running through your head, and these thoughts are known as self-talk. Take steps to prevent yourself from absorbing ideas you don't want or need. When you're not using the television or radio, turn them off and don't let them play in the background. Try to block out the droning babble of the folks in your immediate vicinity. Getting involved in anything that stimulates your creative side is a good way to connect with your id. This can be anything from painting to sculpture, poetry to flower arranging, and photography to dancing.

Improve Your Network's Quality. It's not uncommon for people to feel overwhelmed and unable to focus on anything at all at times. This is the time to reach out to a friend or family member you know well. You may need the assistance of others to go deep within yourself. That's why it's so critical to cultivate a strong professional network; if you can't figure out the problem on your own, your contacts can. In today's fast-paced environment, it can be difficult to maintain a constant sense of self-assurance and support. This is why you need to surround yourself with people who can assist you in discovering your true self. Making the right relationships is critical to your success, so do your research before committing to anyone.

You should also ask yourself difficult questions and answer them truthfully. Despite the difficulty of the exercise, you will already have a conscious answer for each of the questions you will ask. As long as you can access and draw out the most brutally honest replies from your subconscious, you can avoid answering from your conscious mind entirely. In order to accomplish so, how would you go about it? Meditation is the simple solution. Now that these two things are intertwined, you'll need to be honest with yourself about both. Prepare a list of questions to ask yourself, then find a peaceful spot to sit and meditate for a short time. By meditating, you can gain access to your subconscious mind and use it to ask questions to yourself. The more often you practice it, the easier it will be to go deep within yourself and get a better sense of who you are.

No matter if you are awake or asleep, your subconscious mind is constantly at work. Prepare for sleep by studying a few minutes before bedtime. This will help your subconscious mind assimilate information while you are asleep. Keep a dream journal. It's common for the subconscious mind to communicate with you through dreaming. It's time for you to start thinking about the things that truly matter in your life. This way, you'll discover what truly matters to you, and you'll be able to devote your time and energy to things that will help you grow as a person. Keeping in mind that it won't happen in one day is important. The more you do it, the better you will get. Regularly allowing oneself a few moments of solitude will go a long way.

My-mindguide.com

HOW TO BE AWARE OF YOUR INNER COMPASS

Making decisions in line with our values is one of life's most difficult challenges. Decision fatigue is a problem for all of us because of the abundance of information, options, and possibilities that we face. Which counsel should we heed and which should we ignore in the face of so much information? How can we be confident that our choices reflect who we truly are and what we value? Our inner compass is leading us on the right path, but it's up to us to listen to our intuition and act on it.

In today's fast-paced world, our brains are constantly engaged with tasks, deadlines, and dates. There is a growing need to pause, listen, and proceed more thoughtfully, as evidenced by the resurgence of Mindfulness. We are witnessing a worldwide movement to pursue pleasure, meaningful work, and answers to pressing issues that give our lives deeper meaning. There is no simple cure for this problem. There is no one else who can hold the answer, as any excellent practitioner will tell you. As valuable as external support is, it is only a tool to help you think through the issues you confront and dig deeper into your expertise to find the answers to your questions.

These systems of assistance can assist you in putting your knowledge to use in new and innovative ways through guided reflection, learning, and conversation. External supporters may always enable you to learn and improve, which is essential to making better decisions in both your job and personal life, no matter what type of support you choose. Self-work is the other component, and it is the most critical. This is difficult since it is a long-term process that requires a lot of time, effort, and dedication. When we pay attention to our inner voice, we gain a deeper understanding of who we are, our needs, and the cues that guide our decisions.

Every day, set aside time to contemplate. Throughout the day, ask yourself simple questions such as, "How am I feeling?" Is there anything in particular that you enjoyed about today? How would you describe the day's experience as a learning experience for you? What have you discovered? What have you learned about yourself, another person, or the world due to your experience? Even if it's only a few phrases, it's critical that you capture your thoughts in writing. It doesn't matter how long you spend introspecting; journaling helps you consolidate, capture, and face your own self-awareness.

Always be wary about taking advice at face value. We are extremely eager to inquire. Everyone loves to give advice, from family members and friends to coworkers and even your employer. Even though asking questions is usually a good idea, it's easy to get caught up in a cycle of "shoulda-woulda-coulda" rather than taking the time to think things out first. Even if the advice is well-intentioned, it can diminish our ability to think for ourselves, take risks, and rely on our own resources to solve difficulties. Refusing to accept other people's counsel isn't bad, but remember that only you can give the greatest advice.

Our greatest obstacle is fear. Fear of being incorrect, messing up, not being good enough, or worse, facing the 'told you so' song is one of the fundamental reasons we may doubt our capacity to make the right decisions for ourselves. Go out and question those assumptions that prevent you from stepping up instead of accepting failure. If you've always wanted to try your hand at public speaking or take a creative writing class, now is the time. Stop making assumptions and start questioning them. Keep in mind that there are no mistakes but rather great lessons to be learned from them. Make a list of your core principles and stick to them. To you, what matters most is what you believe in. We are who we are because of who we are, what we believe, how we act, and what we think. Many of us have similar values, yet they are all unique to each individual and might change as time goes on. The ability to make decisions based on our most significant wishes and goals is critical at any time, but it is especially critical during times of change or transition.

Learn how to let go. It is easy for us to become bogged down in the idea of how things should be. We may even prevent ourselves from discovering our own truths. Remember that the only constant in life is change, and your experiences, upbringing, socialization, and cultural beliefs all influence your perspective of right and wrong. Almost all of the 'truths' we take for granted today were previously a theory or otherwise considered false at some point in time. When it comes to innovation, creativity, and disruption, it's not enough to think outside the box. It entails examining our preconceived notions, letting go of the chains of the familiar, and adopting an attitude of openness and optimism. Be confident that the answers you seek are within you, waiting for your invitation to come to the forefront of your consciousness. Put your faith in your inner compass so you can discover the wisdom you already possess and live a life of purpose. Ultimately, this is all we really need in life.

Shared Purpose
Mission
Values
Spirit
Vision
Driver
Compensation
Development
Recruiting
Eco-system
Leadership
Followers
Partnership
My-mindguide.com

CHAPTER 3

DO COMPANIES OR BUSINESSES HAVE A SOUL – OR SHOULD THEY?

Products and services from better companies are superior. They create better consumer experiences. Prospects are more likely to choose their brand if these individuals influence them. If they want to charge more, they can. They deliver better margins. Compared to their competitors, their shares have done better in the market. Yes, each and every one of those statements is accurate. That being said, it only provides a partial picture. The flip side of the coin is that better CEOs lead stronger teams. These more successful teams are made up of more invested employees and produce better results. The result is a significant increase in employee satisfaction in the workplace. In order for an entire firm to become a "better organization," there needs to be a higher level of drive. There are no silos, a culture of openness rather than secrecy, and a set of values that encourage effortless productivity.

Elevator pitches are common when you ask a CEO about their company. If you dig deeper, you might uncover the company's purpose statement or philosophy, but you're more likely to come up empty-handed. The soul of a firm, or "company culture," is what distinguishes it as a place to work. In the end, this affects everything from the ability to recruit and retain top talent to the level of productivity and profitability a company achieves. Every great company has a heart. Two things characterize this soul: its basic ideals and its central concentration. I refer to a company's soul as its complete essence—what it stands for and why it exists. In the same way that a person's soul encompasses everything of who they are, a company's soul encompasses all of what it is as well. Most people would describe Apple as an innovative company if given the opportunity to do so in just a few words. Design-conscious. Iconic. Some may even call it espionage. But here's another: Soulful. Yes, Apple has a soul, but it's not the first company to do so. Only a small number of organizations can be claimed to have the kind of "soul" that enthuses their workers and propels them to achieve consistently high levels of organizational performance.

Every business has a goal, a reason for existing, that motivates the products and services it provides. But if no one believes in it, then the purpose is pointless. Through the efforts of these individuals, the company's higher mission is furthered. After interacting with your product or team, buyers are left with a lasting impression of your company's soul. The mind, heart, and conscience of an organization — or even a person — can be viewed as the company's "soul." Mind has the answer. The foundation of an organization's decision-making mechanism is its sense, soul, meaning, and organizational spirit. It is from this perspective that all decisions are or should be made.

It is a company's Soul System that links 'its mission with its overall business strategy and how its employees behave. The concept of sharing is central to this paradigm. A company's culture and success are intimately linked when employees have a common goal, have a common knowledge of the company's strategy, and act in unison.

Every aspect of your business, from where you work to how you set prices, is shaped by the values that define your company's character. Here, trust and openness are a fundamental part of the core principle. The degree to which a person is trustworthy varies from person to person. Some people have an intrinsic suspicion of others, believing that "I will get screwed at every step and have to be forever watchful and careful." "I'm only going to open up to someone who has earned my trust," I say. These policies and processes devalue and disrespect the dignity of employees. Nothing except contempt and an oppressive atmosphere and culture results from it.

For some, believing in the goodness of strangers is normal. Some people may abuse the trust you provide them. To be effective as a leader, you must ensure that all new hires are thoroughly vetted before joining your team. As a result, you require someone capable of working independently; someone who is extremely talented but whose ego does not get in the way when things go wrong, or they are outside of their area of expertise is essential. If you want someone who will do their absolute best for the company's objective, you've found them. When you locate these people and give them your full faith, they will never let you down or betray you.

The soul of your company is like your body; it needs nourishment. The only thing that feeds the soul is the contentment that comes from being successful in one's career and personal life. I believe that everyone should be able to enjoy their free time while working hard, rather than simply working so that they may spend their leisure time. Allowing employees time to pursue personal interests while maintaining a high level of productivity is possible when the culture is high-performing, and trust is high. They don't have to pick one over the other, but they can be relied upon to balance their private lives and their professional ones. Success in both the personal and professional spheres feeds off of one other, allowing employees to work toward both simultaneously. Management has many responsibilities, but the most important one is to help employees achieve their personal and professional goals.

Having a partnership with the Soul of Your Business is like having a trusted business advisor who is always there for you. There's no better way to develop a business that connects with your passion, celebrates your true self, and allows you to give back to others around you than with the guidance of the fundamental truth of your business. In order to build a strong company from the inside out, you must focus on the company's core values. Developing a relationship with the Soul of Your Business will reveal an even more profound diamond at the center of the task that you're here to do. Your business may be built around that, regardless of how well established you are.

TO HAVE A CORPORATE "SOUL" YOU NEED TO:

ENSURE THEY BELIEVE. Millennials are sometimes characterized as having a fanatical adherence to their work, and it's easy to see why. This is not just a generational trait; we all perform better if we believe our work has a greater purpose than just making money. In a corporation with a spirit, there are more than just financial considerations. Its purpose is to make its employees happy and content. It encourages employees to get involved outside of the office and always puts the needs of others ahead of its own bottom line.

Do what it takes to be part of a family. Even though it may sound like a cliché, strong companies and strong families are very much alike. There is always a knowledge that conflict is transient and that nothing can break the bedrock of shared aims, love, and respect in both of these relationships, thus they allow for disagreement and individualism. When life throws a curveball (the non-show nanny, the compassionate leave, the snowstorm-work-from-home days, the crazy customer) over home plate, employers must prove themselves adaptable and supportive of their employees.

TALK. Whether in the workplace or at home, healthy relationships are built on open and honest communication lines. Open and honest feedback is encouraged by good bosses. When left unattended, even the smallest grudges can blossom into something far more serious. From the most junior members of staff to the most senior executives, everyone must be made aware that their thoughts are valid and that their voice may be heard.

INSPIRE. This is when the age-old adage "show, don't tell" comes into play. Your staff won't go the additional mile if you tell them so. Make it clear that you're willing to go above and above for them. In order to be creative, you need to share your own idea process with others. The most important thing you can do for your employees is to set an example of how you want them to conduct themselves in the workplace. 50 percent of American workers have left their employment because they were unhappy in the workplace.

REWARD. If you can't afford it, don't worry. Verbal praise and presents and promotions and raises in pay are more effective rewards for a job well done than money. We're all just like you and me, and we all crave recognition and praise.

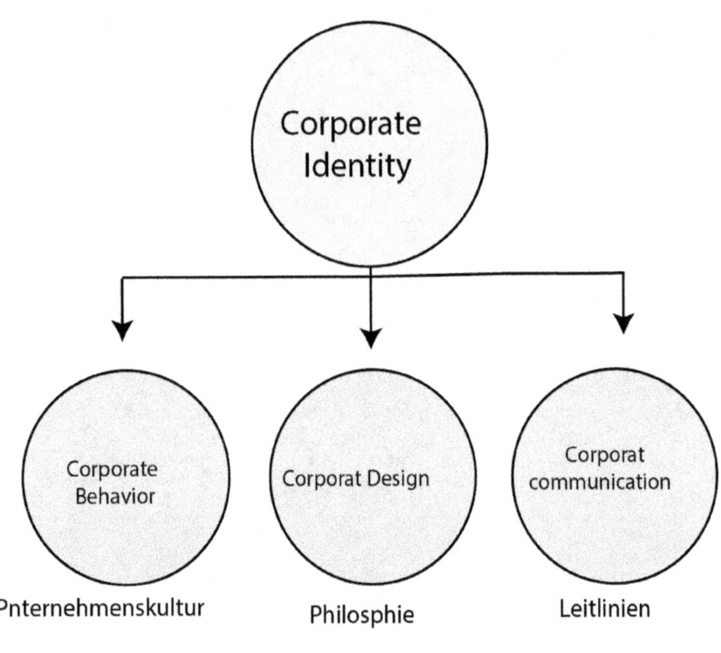

Corporate
Identity
Corporate
Behavior
Corporat Design
Corporat
communication
Pnternehmenskultur
Philosphie
Leitlinien

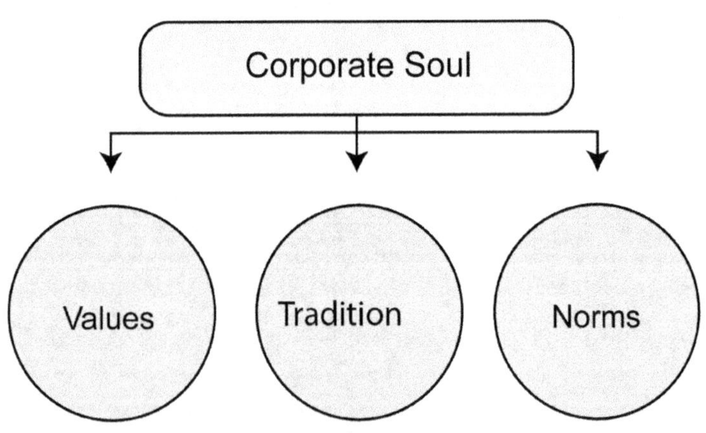

Corporate Soul
Values
Tradition
Norms

My-mindguide.com

UNDERSTANDING WHAT IS A COMPANY'S CORE VALUE (AN ESSENTIAL ELEMENT OF SOUL OF EVERY BUSINESS/CORPORATION)

Companies' core values are defined as clearly expressed principles regarding the organization's vision, goal, and ideals. As a result, all employees, customers, and the greater community are unified around a common goal of providing the best possible service to everyone. That can also be used as a way to describe the culture of a corporation. There is a strong connection between morals and culture. Both deal with a company's loftier goals. The DNA of a corporation is the consequence of this process. Communication inside the company is critical to ensuring that everyone is on the same page. It's a problem that far too many businesses trust their employees know what's most critical. However, having a statement on a wall or website or manual doesn't indicate that employees are receiving the message. There needs to be a consistent flow of information that reaffirms these values.

I'VE FOUND IT USEFUL TO CATEGORIZE VALUES INTO FOUR GROUPS.

As a company's cultural pillars, its CORE VALUES are the fundamental concepts influencing its actions. There can be no compromise on core principles, whether for convenience or short-term financial advantage because they are intrinsic and essential. A company's core beliefs typically reflect the values of its founders; an example of this is HP's lauded "HP Way." In order for a company to stand out, it needs to maintain its identity.

These values a company will need to succeed in the future but do not currently have adapting to the demands of an evolving market or sector may need creating a new value for a company. An aspirational value was used in place of a core value by the CEO, who said that his company's core value was a sense of urgency. In order to avoid diluting the basic values, aspirational values must be handled appropriately. When I worked for one company, staff were known to work late into the night and on weekends because they were valued for their dedication and hard work. To avoid confusion among employees, executives opted against adding the aspirational value of "work-life balance" to the company's list of values because they feared that doing so would confuse them.

PERMISSION-TO-PLAY VALUES simply reflect the basic behavioral and social standards that must be met by every employee. They don't differ greatly between businesses, especially those in the same region or industry, therefore they don't, by definition, help a business stand out from its rivals.

As time goes on, these values take hold of the organization without being nurtured by leadership. Employees' interests and personalities are often reflected in these items. Accidental ideals, such as fostering a culture of inclusion, might benefit a business. However, they might also act as a barrier to fresh possibilities. Managers must be able to tell the difference between essential principles and those that are simply coincidental.

EXAMPLES OF KEY VALUES AT WORK

Company values can be summarized as the Golden Rule if reduced to their simplest form. Put yourself in the other person's shoes and treat them the same way you would like to be treated. Its core ideals can define an organization's soul.

Integrity. Everyone who represents the organization and the company as a whole must act with high ethics.

Honesty. It's more than just the wisest choice. Being open and honest with one's coworkers, clients, and the general public is an important part of doing business.

Fairness. Everyone should be treated with the respect and decency that we as a society are entitled to and expect.

Accountability. Self-reflection is the most effective technique to create trust both internally and externally.

Customers are promised. A great customer experience begins with being genuine to the words we use and the ties we establish with our clients and colleagues.

Diversity & Inclusion. An organization's success is based on its ability to bring together people from various backgrounds and experiences in a common environment.

Learning. The truth is that no one knows everything. The foundation of any successful company is a spirit of openness and curiosity.

Teamwork. Together, people can do things that they couldn't have done alone.

Passion. Joy in the work itself and the people around us so that we can all be daring and creative together.

Quality. Products and services are judged by their craftsmanship. Therefore, companies need to maintain the highest standards.

HOW TO DEFINE YOUR COMPANY VALUES

An in-depth look at the culture and vision of your firm is necessary to define your company values. It's important to reflect on how your company's values might help communicate its mission and vision. Your staff should be able to easily remember and embody your company's core beliefs. Instead of writing an essay, ponder the deeper significance of your ideals. Make them understandable to the average person by simplifying them into terms they can follow. It's also unclear and dilutes your meaning to write in corporate jargon. Your company's values must be tied to its mission and ambitions. They should be relevant to your company's products and services, as well as its culture.

Address both your internal and exterior objectives at the same time. When a firm makes decisions, they not only affect its employees, but also have an impact on the world. Disingenuous to ignore the impact your organization has on the outside world. Your company's staff will feel encouraged, and your consumers will have more faith in your ability to communicate with the outside world.

Make them stand out from the crowd. If you're following the same set of values as another firm or even a competitor, you'll be seen as a copycat and lose customers. Be specific about what sets your company apart from the competition, then use your company values to communicate that message. After you've established your principles, you need to incorporate them into your company's culture. Recognizing employees that exemplify your company values is a great approach to creating a culture in line with those principles. Employees are more likely to repeat an action if the company has already recognized it. Clearly connecting appreciation to the organization's ideals enhances the alignment between the company and its employees.

If your firm encourages everyone in your organization—from your employees to your executives—to practice frequent praise, it will strengthen your organization's values and lead to higher performance across the board. Consider implementing a platform for employee recognition that allows employees to clearly link each recognition to a specific company value in order to simplify the recognition process.

VALUES CLAIMED ARE NOT VALUES LIVED UP (THE VALUE GAP) BY MOST ORGANIZATIONS

Leaders are well aware that company values statements are frequently used as a gimmick. They don't seem to see the damaging effects of allowing this to happen, which is surprising. There's an automatic grab for the cultural lever, as if creating and disseminating an ethical code has any sort of impact. They are taken aback when the organization's response is one of cynicism, hostility, and then, finally, indifference. A company's value statements become nothing more than a showpiece. Employee cynicism and low morale result from values that have been appropriated and abused. There are numerous ways in which this can happen. As a result, any fruitful discussion is stifled by using values as a political weapon. Values can also be employed to divert attention away from wrongdoing and create the appearance of progress when, in fact, little progress has been made.

There are several reasons why it is a pity when values are devalued, but the most important one is that it robs us of a chance. There are several ways in which a company's values can be used to differentiate it from its competitors. But establishing and enforcing a set of strong values requires a lot of courage. Because values are painful when effectively implemented, every company looking to implement a values-based project needs to accept this fact first. Some employees are made to feel like outsiders by them. Strategic and operational freedom are constrained, as are the actions of the organization's employees. Because of this, executives face a barrage of criticism for even minor transgressions. Constant monitoring is required. Making a values statement is a waste of time if you cannot embrace the sacrifices that true principles entail. The absence of one will be beneficial to your situation. However, it is possible to acquire vital lessons from a few organizations that have adopted relevant corporate values by persevering through the task. Although these organizations' values may have been derived directly from their founders' vision and character through formal training programs, they all followed four key imperatives in defining and applying their values.

In reality, the basic principles of most organizations are just aspirational goals for the future. Executives frequently misinterpret other values for core principles. Employees are baffled by the jumble that results, and management appears out of touch as a result. This will ensure that everyone understands what the company is trying to accomplish by establishing some fundamental terms that everyone can agree on. In reality, some employees see corporate principles as meaningless blather that don't influence how business is done on a daily basis.

One of the principles of a firm is to create an environment where employees can maintain a healthy work-life balance. A few after-hours and weekend meeting times will be set aside. As a result, employees will doubt whether or not this company cares about achieving a work-life balance. Employees grow skeptical and lose faith in their leaders if they believe their company isn't living true to its proclaimed values. Employee morale suffers due to a lack of faith in upper management. In the same way that a web of trust takes time and effort to weave, so too can a single blow demolish it.

HOW TO MEASURE YOUR ORGANIZATIONAL CULTURE AND VALUES

In order to accomplish difficult tasks as quickly and efficiently as possible, company executives always want to ensure that their staff works together as a team. The company's culture is shaped by various elements, such as cooperation among employees, interpersonal ties inside the company, and job satisfaction. Any leader must consider the culture of their organization. Organizational culture and values that permeate the workplace are critical to determining how a firm functions and, conversely, determining how it might improve.

As part of the high-performance, values-aligned culture, a set of measurable, tangible, and observable corporate core values is essential. As long as values aren't measurable, it's impossible to consistently hold leaders and employees accountable for them. Often, values are stated in lofty words that are difficult to put into practice on a day-to-day basis. Each leader and employee can define these principles as they see fit, depending on their personality, role, and responsibilities, without explicit behavioral norms, which describe exactly how a "great corporate citizen" behaves. I lose faith in you if you don't act following my definition of "honesty," for example. Long-term effects? Increased tension and anxiety among personnel and clients and inconsistent handling of both.

Create a list of possible behaviors that you'd want to see your employees exhibit while they're modeling each of the company's core values. You can't hold people accountable for what they "think," what their "attitude" is, or what they "believe," but you can hold them accountable for displaying (acting on) clearly defined behaviors.

Twice a year, conduct a custom values assessment of the entire organization. As many channels as possible should be used to disseminate information on the organization's progress toward its goal of "representing our beliefs." Pay attention to the people who are showing the ideal values, and reward them for their efforts while coaching and redirecting those who aren't. As soon as you discover employees who are incapable of regularly demonstrating the desired valued behaviors, kindly assist them in leaving the company.

COMMUNICATING YOUR COMPANY'S VALUES

What are your company's internal ways of expressing its values? Even the most well-thought-out mission statements are of no use if they are kept under wraps and rarely brought to employees' attention. Everybody should be able to see a company's essential ideals, which should be displayed prominently on the company's main stage. Effective communication inside an organization accomplishes precisely that goal. Repetition of business values reminds everyone what makes the company special and distinct. Everything a company does is a statement of its values. Consider the following examples of how a company's daily operations can be influenced by its core values:

Consider Others: Identify those who will be involved in developing your core values before you begin. Leadership and staff may form a small or large coalition, depending on the size of your team. If practicable, consider inviting staff from different departments or levels to participate in the brainstorming session. Having an open, anonymous brainstorm where employees can contribute ideas for improving their firm's value is another option to investigate. These strategies can increase employee ownership of these assets by casting a wide net during the creation process.

Once the coalition has been formed, all members must be on the same page when it comes to implementing the plan. They should be willing to brainstorm and compromise in order to come up with and execute these ideals, and they should be able to display these attributes themselves. A member of the team needs to be able to voice their concerns about one of the principles so that the group can come to a compromise. Members of the alliance must also be committed to living these principles themselves if they hope to inspire others. If leadership doesn't "walk the walk" of the organization's principles, employees will have a hard time following them and may even despise them.

Your company's principles should also be reflected in its culture. These two notions generally link successful and unsuccessful companies, and they can both have a direct impact on their success or failure. If they are not developed in accordance with the company's culture, organizational values may fall short of the mark. This is mostly due to the fact that they are perceived as being untrue to the "feel" of the workplace by many employees. Many of today's top corporations, like Google, have incorporated culture into their core beliefs. You will have a better chance of enlisting aid in applying your values if they appear to be genuine to you. Why is it important to examine the relationship between your company's culture and its values, then? Begin by asking a few simple questions. What components of your company's culture are most important to you? What are the most important attributes to look for in a new employee or a new customer? It is important to think about what aspects of your business or corporate culture will be relevant to the dialogue. Think about how each of these defines your organization.

Be Aggressively Authentic: Many firms treat a values initiative like a marketing launch: a one-time event assessed by the early attention it generates, not by the validity of its content. A company's leaders' reputation can be eroded by this, as the CEO of a financial services firm realized when he displayed a fake film. Companies can be sabotaged even by leaders who take values initiatives seriously because blandly pleasant principles fail to set them apart from their competition. In many firms' values statements, you'll find the motherhood-and-apple-pie ideals of honesty, fairness, and excellence in service to customers. In fact, 55% of Fortune 100 businesses say that integrity is a core value, 49% believe in customer satisfaction, and 40% believe in teamwork. However, such phrases do not provide a clear pattern for how employees should behave. Because cookie-cutter ideals don't make a company stand out from the rest of the pack, they instead make it blend in. As long as the words don't sound like they belong on a Hallmark card, the statement is sincere. Indeed, some of the most value-driven organizations adhere to challenging, if not outright contentious, principles. It is possible to make smart decisions by aggressively adhering to your core ideals.

For example, Intel takes great satisfaction in the more abrasive features of their corporate culture. Risk-taking encourages employees to challenge the status quo and engage in constructive conflict. For example, the art of verbal sparring without harboring grudges is taught to new hires as part of the company's orientation program. When it comes to meetings, Andy Grove is known for challenging and even berating his executives. During a presentation, Grove's former direct reports remember the former CEO chastising them. Following an initial pause, Grove said, "If this doesn't get more fascinating, you might want to stop right now and come back next week with a better narrative." Grove had halted the executive's speech just a few minutes earlier.

It is possible to make smart decisions by aggressively adhering to your core ideals. So, when San Francisco Bay Area-based Webcor Builders decided to buy a vendor, a consulting firm that wired construction firms with high-bandwidth technology, they utilized their core value of innovation as a compass for their strategy. The acquisition could have seemed like a risky move for a bricks-and-mortar construction company, but it paid off. Architects and engineers who previously had to rely on phone calls and cumbersome plans may now work together online, saving time and money. The decision was influenced as much by our commitment to innovation as it was by market conditions.

Own the Method: To begin a values initiative, what is the most common first step taken by many CEOs? As a result, HR is free to use this endeavor to promote diversity and inclusion in other ways. With the help of surveys and town hall meetings, Human Resources (HR) works to keep employees engaged.

In other words, that's exactly the incorrect strategy to take. Rather than fostering consensus, values campaigns aim to impose a set of core, strategically sound beliefs on a large number of individuals. Consensus-based decision-making can be dangerous when it comes to strategy, money, and other business concerns, but leaders appear blind to the danger when it comes to building values. If you want to know what your employees think about your company's values, you shouldn't ask them. Firstly, it incorporates ideas from a large number of people who may or may not have a role at the company. This generates the idea that every input is of equal value, and it is also misleading.

Rather than fostering agreement, values campaigns aim to impose a set of fundamental, strategic beliefs on a large number of individuals. Observe what happened when a technology company's CEO allowed the HR department to spearhead a values campaign. In the wake of numerous meetings and polls, he agreed without hesitation that collaboration should be one of the company's values. But just a few weeks later, he fully disavowed this principle by saying, "I don't really believe in teams; I feel that achievement occurs when individuals work individually." Managers were understandably perplexed and dismayed by the results of the study. In the words of a former senior executive, "The distance between what we were saying and what we were doing was just too great."

It's preferable to work with a small team that includes the CEO, any company founders still employed, and a few important staff. The CEO of a pharmaceutical company understood better than to make the discussion of values a democratic process since he wanted his company to have a distinct culture. To achieve his goals, Wild relied on a team of seven senior executives, many of whom were instrumental in the company's inception. Some of MedPointe's employees were singled out by the company's leaders as exemplars of the ideals the company should uphold. Employees who cannot embrace or exemplify these ideals will be accommodated, says Wild. At a different company, they may be a better fit." The highest-ranking executives must also realize that a strong values program is like a superb wine: it must be savored slowly. An effective declaration is more crucial for a values team than a decision that it may regret later. As a result, executives should take their time to think about how the standards they set will be implemented in their workplaces.

After a series of acquisitions, an international pharmaceutical business found that allowing time for reflection was useful in creating a unified culture. They nearly agreed on a list of values that included "transparent" after just a few hours of discussion because they wanted to move on to other issues. Plan: CEO wisely tabled the proposal so that the team may ponder and evaluate it with key staff members. Before finalizing it, they noticed that the term had a different meaning in Europe than it did in the United States. The team changed the word "transparent" to "collaborative," and as a result, the chosen values were far more in line with the worldwide ethos of the company.

Let's assume you've figured out the right values. Now what? What's going to happen next? If you want your core values to stick, you'll need to incorporate them into every aspect of managing your workforce, from hiring practices to performance evaluations to criteria for awards and promotions to procedures for terminating workers. Everyone in the organization should know the company's basic principles at all times, not only during interviews but throughout their employment. Let's take a look at Cussions and Cussions (fictitious), a small e-business organization that has effectively built a strong culture around dependability, dedication, and self-motivation by integrating these fundamental principles into every system that directly impacts its employees. When it comes to hiring, employers look for individuals who have the qualifications and experience needed for the position and have the character traits that reflect the company's core values. During interviews, the CEO and his staff will inquire candidly about job expectations and prior successes. As an example of how the CEO measures a candidate's drive and commitment, candidates are asked to describe something they've accomplished that others had written off as unattainable.

The company's ideals aren't simply words for Cussions and Cussion's employees after they arrive. Core values are used as a basis for evaluating employees and awarding shares, incentives, and raises to the CEO and his staff. A person's values even inform the decision to fire them or not. The CEO would say, "I can deal with someone who needs more counseling or training, but when it comes to our essential beliefs, I have to be intolerant." Because of this, our culture is solid. "Many organizations avoid having to lay off employees because they have strong cultures like this one. With Baker's Delight, another example may be given (fictitious). After just a few days, it's hard for a new employee to fail to see the importance of client happiness. Every bakery room is named after a client, and the artwork on the walls originates from the customers' annual reports. Auditor-independent assessments of customer satisfaction are used to award bonuses and compensation plans. At every opportunity, a business should be promoting its core principles. Unless bosses repeat a message seven times, employees, it is thought, will not believe what they are told. Since so many people are skeptical of values today, executives should recite them whenever possible.

A lot of organizations put their principles on T-shirts and coffee mugs, but the most effective ways to communicate them are far less expensive and time-consuming. It's critical that you keep reminding your personnel of the company's primary value of customer service at all times. An alternative to a comprehensive manual on how to provide excellent customer service is telling your new hires extravagant stories about the extent to which other employees have gone for them to be impressed by their clients. You can tell them the story of a representative who returned a customer's long-purchased products and made a refund with no questions asked. Employees' opinion that they work for a great firm is reinforced by the stories they hear over and over. When the store is closed, managers should examine both positive and negative feedback from customers to understand how their employees are performing.

It's no secret that Wal-Mart is one of the most practical businesses on the planet, but it's also one of the most recognizable. Employees at the retail behemoth are frequently reminded of the company's basic principles of quality, customer service, and respect. In Europe, we think of things like cheers as typical of American naivete, as one management trainee explained to me. The posters in the break room and the Sam Walton statements we read about aren't stupid at all, I must admit." Managers utilize action to reinforce key principles. Workers who come up with innovative ways to serve consumers, for example, have traditionally received cash and other public accolades. Developing and executing a strong values system takes a lot of time and effort, and most firms would rather not bother. Indeed, they should not, because a company's culture can be infected by values that haven't been properly established.

It's challenging to live up to the proclaimed values of your company. Even if giving in to politically correct pressures is easier, being honest and unapologetic about what you believe is considerably more difficult still. Repairing the harm done by faulty value programs is much more difficult for businesses. Even while it may take some time and effort to create an authentic values statement, it's a good bet that your firm will benefit greatly from it.

Summarily, make a difference by including people in creating company values. Involve your employees, customers, stockholders, and other key stakeholders. The entire organization must embrace the ideals, and management must be on board. Commitment to principle begins at the top. They must consider the business principles when making critical decisions and allude to them when explaining why these decisions were made. Be reasonable with your expectations. Employees should be informed by management that they should strive to operate in accordance with the company's values but that it may not always be possible to achieve this. Sometimes it's inevitable, but an exception needs to be made for meetings to be held on Saturdays and Sundays, as well.

Make sure your company's values are up-to-date. As the marketplace shifts, organizations must constantly adapt to be relevant. The company's values need to be updated as necessary to keep up with the times. Keep an eye on the organization's ideals and how they are being implemented. To ensure that its activities align with its stated values, management should set aside regular intervals of time to conduct such evaluations. Employees should also be surveyed to see if they think the organization is living up to its ideals. A company's values can be codified in a way that is beneficial to it. Depending on their alignment, leadership and employees can use the values as a solid foundation for their actions and decisions. The most important thing is that everyone commits to living according to the values.

CHAPTER 5

DEFINING AND EXPLORING BRAND VALUE MEANS SOUL SEARCHING – DIVE DEEPER

An overall company's brand makes up the product's name and appearance. Although the same parent firm owns many brands, they all have unique visions, messages, products, target markets, and sets of brand values that define them from one another. Brand values are vital to today's successful brands. Brands that succeed tend to have a well-defined set of values that impact practically every aspect of their operations. Like someone's personal beliefs, a brand should remain consistent with retaining a distinct identity and a devoted customer base.

Brand values can be discovered by considering your company as a whole. When it comes to branding, several external elements make up your identity, including your tone of voice and personality and your visual identity. However, the "internal" aspect of your brand genuinely affects your customer connections by building sentiments of familiarity and affinity between you and your customers. An integral part of your marketing mix is the "brand values" element, which directs your company's mission, identity, and value proposition. As we all know, the most memorable brands win the most customers because they have a clear value proposition for their brand's target audience. It is important to have a well-thought-out plan for communicating your brand's values, as well as a well-defined brand culture and community.

In other words, they are the basic values that you, as a business, stand for in everything you do. They guide your brand story, actions, behaviors, and decision-making process. You will have to make difficult decisions in business. It's easier to make the proper decision if you have core principles that consistently remind you of what matters most to your organization and to the people you serve. It's also nice to know that your decisions are based on values that are in line with your company's overall mission and vision. This should be obvious, but your brand values definition should be a unique expression of your company's culture and identity. You can't simply copy and paste from another company's successful strategy. For inspiration, look to powerful firms but make sure that your basic values are reflected in your DNA.

As a business, you live by your brand values. As a business, you can't do anything without a strong brand identity. It influences everything from how you communicate to your decisions about your company's future. A company's culture and client base are shaped in part by its brand values. This company's basic beliefs should resonate with customers and employees alike. In order to distinguish a company's brand from its competitors, its values should be a unique and unforgettable representation of what's at its core, as well.

Authenticity and transparency are the hallmarks of a great brand value. The terms "vague" and "value" don't frequently appear in the same sentence. Make sure that your brand's values are easily understood when choosing the principles to base it on. While Netflix uses a slideshow to communicate their ideals, Buffer uses bullet points to convey their ideas. They choose ideals consistent with who they are as a company and who they want to be. For both customers and employees, it's important to know exactly what a company stands for and how it applies those values to its daily operations. Keep in mind that your brand's values aren't about your product or service as you begin developing your own. "Quality" is easy to express if you have a valued physical thing to sell. But merely producing the best chocolate bar on the market isn't enough to keep customers coming back for more. Alternatively, even if you provide the most user-friendly SaaS solution on the B2B market, it does not ensure that your users renew their subscriptions. A closer connection with your customers will help them remember you and return for more.

Your brand's values should not mutate along with your customers or the organizations they work for. If you're witnessing many negative reactions to your current code of ethics, it's time to reassess. Make your scruples something that may develop and change with you over time, and make sure that you stick to your guns. Branding is more than simply providing an excellent product or service. For a company to be successful, it must establish trust with the people it serves. One of the best ways to keep customers loyal to a business is to make them feel like they're part of the family. The core values of a company are embodied in the products and services they offer and the way they conduct business. In order to communicate these values to your audience, you must first identify and record these fundamental values. However, many organizations don't take the time to establish and document these values, or they don't delve deep enough when creating their company brand values. The process of determining your unique brand value might be frustrating. Not describing your goals or how and why you aim to accomplish them. An alternative approach focuses on how your brand will behave as long as you serve your target market. To break that pledge would be catastrophic. It's a waste of time and money to use terms that appear to have been plucked from a dictionary at random. Customers will connect with a company if it has basic principles that it is ready to fight for.

WHY BRAND VALUES ARE IMPORTANT

There is a lot more to a brand than just your products or services. Your brand is a statement of who you are and what you believe in. One thing that should never change: your brand values. Your logo, products, website, and even digital marketing strategies can all alter over time. A company's overall brand identity must have a strong set of brand values. Your brand identity's visual and linguistic parts (logo, colors, and typefaces) are critical to attracting your target audience. However, it is via your company's underlying brand values that you can build long-term relationships with your customers. Consumers' perceptions of your brand are strongly influenced by its basic principles. In today's market, consumers are looking for brands that match themselves with their beliefs. So it's critical to not only develop your brand values but also communicate them to your customers.

Customers today expect more from their favorite brands than just an eye-catching logo or a well-designed website, and firms must meet this need by providing a deeper level of consumer engagement. It's your brand values, not your brand's name or voice, that create true connections with your customers.

HOW TO DISCOVER THE UNIQUE SELLING PROPOSITION OF YOUR BRAND

As tempting as it is to think of your brand value statement as a chance to brag, there is a lot more to a company's beliefs than a set of powerful words and phrases. If you want to give your brand values definition the impact it needs, you can't just tell people that your firm is generous, thoughtful, and environmentally conscious. How do you know what a company stands for? To be successful in your business, you must consider what is most important not only to yourself, but also to your coworkers, stockholders, investors, and consumers. Because they reflect client beliefs while also embracing the company's passions, successful examples of brand value are hard to come by.

In order to begin the process of discovering your brand's essential principles, you'll need to move beyond the pre-existing box of generic company phrases. It sounds good, but it doesn't capture the essence of what makes your company special and influential. Consider what you're passionate about instead of idealized terminology if you'd like your brand principles to help you stand out. Does your organization care about its customers? If so, you're in the right place. Want to do your part to protect the environment and make a difference? Organize your coworkers and customers around a set of shared ideas that you believe in.

Try to think about your customers' requirements and expectations objectively while also keeping in mind what your competitors have to offer. To better stand out from the competition, you could benefit from conducting an initial competitor analysis to see whether or not there is a need for your product or service. Those values that address a current market demand have the most impact on a company's brand. Consider what your clients already believe and their expectations from their favorite companies rather than trying to convince them to feel the same way you do about a certain notion.

Stand up for what you believe in! In what words would your consumers describe you to a potential customer? Is your customer service regarded as exceptional? Won't they tell their friends that you have the lowest prices or the highest quality products outside of the UK? Try to build brand values around what buyers currently associate with your organization. Personalized customer service and email marketing, for example, can help you build a strong brand by demonstrating your desire to go the extra mile for your clients. Then, with everything you've got, fight for it. Try to think outside the box to enhance the client experience. A brand's value proposition, as previously stated, should not change over time. In order to have the best chance of gaining real brand loyalty, you need to stick to your core values, even if they change over time.

Your brand values description should be pared down to a few essential words and phrases that may be used as a guide for your business team when they need it most. In order to maintain a consistent brand image across all mediums, your employees must be well-versed in your core principles in order to do their jobs effectively. Next, you'll need to figure out how to incorporate your basic beliefs into your company's structure. Brand values should be consistent throughout all of your marketing and branding initiatives. Make sure that your basic principles are reflected in your customer engagement approach. A hypocrite is despised by all, including the stock market.

As long as you don't act in accordance with your fundamental beliefs, you won't be able to build brand loyalty in customers, which isn't a good plan. Your core principles should guide every decision your firm takes. Whenever you and the other decision-makers in your company are discussing a choice, ask yourself and them how well a specific decision is aligned with your firm's values. From the bottom to the top, your company's culture should be shaped by your beliefs. They should be an integral component of your company's operations. As a manager, you want your employees to know and use your values in everything they do. As an explanation for behavior, values should provide an explanation that goes beyond the realm of choice. Value propositions with this kind of universal functionality may not be the ideal fit for your firm.

EXAMPLES OF COMPANIES WITH KILLER CORE VALUES

As a manager, you must establish a set of basic principles that everyone can agree on and rally around. And there's no better place to begin than by studying successful examples of other organizations. Because, after all, some of the world's most well-known businesses were able to rise to the top because they were able to communicate their company values in the most effective way possible. The value proposition of Apple, Coca-Cola, Nike, and other well-known brands has enabled these companies to develop a marketing strategy that has been well received by their target market. This is a good time to ask yourself a few questions about the values that distinguish some of your favorite businesses and brands. Let's examine what we can learn from some of the best examples of corporate core principles from some of the most well-known companies.

APPLE CORE VALUES: For decades, Apple has been known for its creative and forward-thinking products and services. There have been a few setbacks along the route to success, however. Apple developed the "Think Different" campaign in 1997 to make its brand principles clear to its target audience, employees, and shareholders alike. "Think Different" demonstrated that Apple's goal is to create world-class products while keeping technology accessible to the general public. Apple is known for its quality over quantity mentality, which is reflected in the company's brand values. In today's world, Apple employees are more cohesive than ever before, producing seamless experiences for customers both online and off.

NIKE'S CORE VALUES: "Just do it" is a recurring theme in Nike's brand values. The tagline was originally intended to combat the rising tide of obesity in the United States, but it also represents the company's values of heroism and ambition. We want to inspire and innovate for every athlete on our planet," Nike states in its mission statement. It is also stated that everybody with a physique is considered an athlete by Nike's brand standards. As a result, Nike is all about promoting achievement, motivating athletes, and reminding everyone that they can achieve their goals.

ADIDAS CORE VALUES: As one might expect from one of the world's biggest sports equipment producers, Adidas places its basic principles in the context of a competition, emphasizing, among other things, that "we play to win." Here are Adidas' key values:

Purpose: Through sport, we have the power to change lives.

Mission: To be the best sports company in the world.

A deeper dive: "Athletes will not settle for average. And neither do we. We have a clear mission: To be the best sports company in the world. Every day, we come to work to create and sell the best sports and fitness products in the world, and to offer the best service and consumer experience—and to do it all in a sustainable way. To successfully do that, we focus entirely on our authentic sports brands as they connect and engage with our consumers." It's all about winning—improving their competitive position, achieving peak performance—and, in that, Adidas' values match those of their customers.

KELLOGG'S CORE VALUES: Another iconic American brand is Kellogg's. Each one of Kellogg's six core values represents what kind of people they want to hire and the businesses they want to partner with, as well as what kind of products they want to make available to their customers. Due to Kellogg's dedication to its core values, the company has received numerous honors. According to Black Enterprise, Kellogg's was one of the 50 best companies for diversity, and it was also included in the Diversity, Inc. lists of the top 50 companies for veterans and LGBT employees in 2018. In addition, the US Environmental Protection Agency named Kellogg a 2030 Food Loss & Waste Champion, and Ethisphere named Kellogg a World's Most Ethical Company.

Having thousands of employees around the world, Kellogg needed to make sure they were aligned with their company's goals. When Melissa Howell, Kellogg's Chief Human Resources Officer, explains how they accomplished this: "We need to figure out a way to get our staff on board with the Kellogg's goal. Reinforcing behaviors and reinforcing success is one of the most important aspects. Because everyone can see how Kellogg's employees are modeling the habits that contribute to our success, a global recognition platform is a great method to achieve this goal." Over 80,000 employee recognitions have been issued to Kellogg's in the first four months of using Achievers. The platform made it simple for everyone to identify coworkers who exemplify successful conduct while also reinforcing Kellogg's principles of fairness and inclusion.

JOHN LEWIS CORE VALUES: When creating a strong brand value proposition, John Lewis is an expert. John Lewis has established one of the most cherished retail brands in the United Kingdom thanks to its unwavering commitment to its brand principles. The company's founder, John Spedan Lewis, established that the corporation should focus on purpose, profit, power, members, and commercial partnerships from the very beginning.. That may sound vague, but the John Lewis brand values have driven the company to become a corporation that values its partners and employees above all else. It's a win-win situation for everyone involved! The John Lewis slogan "Never knowingly undersold" ensures that John Lewis retains the respect and love of its fans.

VIRGIN MEDIA CORE VALUES: There may be no better example of brand values than Virgin Media today. A student newspaper is said to have been the origin of the Virgin name in the 1970s. Virgin founder Richard Branson has quickly expanded his reach into the retail and record industries as well as launching an airline. However, despite Virgin Media's rapid expansion, the "big man" Richard Branson has maintained a firm grasp on six key values that guide the company's operations. Giving value for money (never be cheap), offering quality and attention to detail (but not at the expense of affordability), and innovation are some of our core beliefs (always hire professional, empowered people capable of giving a great experience).

GOOGLE CORE VALUES: When it comes to Google's basic values, "don't be evil" is a well-known one. Google's values can be summarized in this way. However, it does not tell the complete story. To sum up, Google holds the following values:

Focus on the user, and all else will follow.
It's best to do one thing really, really well.
Fast is better than slow.
Democracy on the web works.
You don't need to be at your desk to need an answer.
You can make money without doing evil.
There's always more information out there.
The need for information crosses all borders.
You can be serious without a suit.
Great just isn't good enough.

Google's priorities are a little different because it is a technological corporation. In the same way that you won't find Adidas or Google worried about sports performance, you won't find them worrying about how well democracy works on the internet. Their tone, which is less formal and more philosophical, also reflects the values of the industry (and the corporation itself). You can use the phrase as both a TED talk title and a core principle for your business: "You can make money without doing evil." This shows that Google appreciates its employees highly and holds them to the highest standards of conduct. To guarantee that their values are still relevant to the firm's aims and mission, Google has re-evaluated its values numerous times since the company was just a few years old.

BMW BRAND VALUES: It's common for BMW customers to link the brand with high-end products and services. An important part of BMW's brand identity is tied to the company's goods. On the other hand, BMW has made a concerted effort to project an image of luxury with their vehicles. The core of the BMW brand's ideals is to provide the automobile industry with the best goods and services. BMW isn't simply a car company; they're a driving experience company. To uphold these beliefs, the company asks customers for input on a regular basis and holds them accountable for their performance. They also emphasize Integrity, Responsibility, Growth, and Respect in their daily operations and marketing (treating each customer with dignity and courtesy). The combination of these brand principles creates the idea of a fully sophisticated brand.

STARBUCKS CORE VALUES: Coffee may be found almost anywhere, from gas stations to fast food joints to the Keurig machine in your office. One reason Starbucks is so great is that they took something that was essentially a commodity and turned it into a luxury version and the market leader. Their essential ideals serve as a road map for success. "We live these values with our partners, our coffee, and our customers at our core:

Creating a culture of warmth and belonging, where everyone is welcome.

Acting with courage, challenging the status quo and finding new ways to grow our company and each other.

Being present, connecting with transparency, dignity and respect.

Delivering our very best in all we do, holding ourselves accountable for results.

We are performance driven, through the lens of humanity."

There are those who believe that Starbucks' success might be attributed to the culture and atmosphere of their stores. As the company's executive chairman and previous CEO, Howard Schultz, put it, "We're in the business of human connection and humanity." Throughout the firm's ideals, even when discussing financial outcomes and company growth, the tone is cheerful and almost familial, reflecting Starbucks' community-oriented business approach.

LEGO BRAND VALUES: When you think of Lego, what comes to mind? Creativity? Fun? The toys are of high quality? The fact that this is the case isn't a fluke. Lego aspired to be more than a toy maker for children. A highly competitive market necessitated that they find ways to differentiate themselves by providing products and services that their target audience valued. As a toy corporation, Lego's brand values revolve around innovation, fun, and imagination. On the other hand, Lego goes a step further by emphasizing ideals that are appealing to both parents and children. For example, their toys offer "learning" possibilities, excellent customer service, and a high standard of craftsmanship. Lego is the world's leading manufacturer of children's toys because of its distinctive brand values.

KEYTAKEAWAY: One thing your company should never do is simply steal the core values of a more established business and use them as yours. While you may have certain principles in common with other businesses, you must take the time to reflect on who you are as a company and what you actually stand for before moving forward. Someone else's work cannot be used as a substitute for one of your own. Observing how other businesses describe themselves is critical. Learn how crucial it is for your company's values to exist in the language your customers and prospects use. When it comes to setting your values, it's vital to think about what's important to you rather than what other people might like to hear. For example, you may observe how the industry you work in has its own set of values and how those values may influence what you choose to stress. You can see how your beliefs and the way you live them may turn your product from a commodity to a crucial one. 'You may rest assured that if you need to present a certain image in your sector, you can get away with having simple, straight-laced values. When revising or creating your own core principles, look to these brands for inspiration. For some, it could be just what they've been looking for.

REPUTATION IS THE GUARDIAN OF A COMPANY'S BRAND

Your brand can aid your business, but it's less clear how that personal brand might help you achieve your personal and professional goals. Your reputation is the foundation of your brand. People talk about you when you're not there. If you run a tiny business or a large corporation, this is true regardless of the size of your organization. Good things stated about us in our absence have a positive effect on us all: opportunities arise, people work with us more effectively and word of mouth conducts our marketing for us. Are you putting yourself in such a way as to produce an impression that stands out in the midst of all the other noise? What is it about you that sticks in their craw? People won't fit you into a box with everyone else in your sector if you have a unique perspective.

Brand reputation is the X-factor that enables your firm to charge profitable rates, generate customer loyalty, and create a winning team culture that encourages employees to serve consumers and expand the business. The best aspect is that no one can buy your good name. A preoccupation with providing excellent customer service is a prerequisite. A successful business understands that their product or service is more than just a transaction: they're in the relationship business. Everybody has a compelling benefit, voice, or imagery in today's world. Despite this, a brand's reputation must be earned. Because of this, it has a higher level of credibility. Since your customers and staff have so many friends and family members who trust them, it's easier to scale.

As much time as you put into perfecting your message, your brand is ultimately in your customer's hands. What your customers think, feel, and remember about you is what makes up your brand. Whatever you claim to be in your branding and marketing activities is meaningless. It doesn't matter what your consumers think of you; whatever they think of you is what you are. You don't have to fight your brand reputation when it comes to great branding. If you can master this skill, you'll be able to align your brand with the perceptions of others. Finally, what really counts is how people perceive the brand because its success or failure will be based on how many people want to utilize its products or services.

Assuming your product or service even moderately lives up to the hype, a high brand reputation will also create a form of social pressure for people to share their experiences with your product or service. Because people want to be regarded as savvy and well-informed, having a good reputation is a win-win situation for your business. No matter how amazing a product or service is, a company with a terrible brand reputation will struggle to make sales. A poor association with your brand will keep customers away from your product altogether. If, on the other hand, the brand has a great reputation, they will have more room to maneuver, even if they occasionally underperform. Apple serves as an obvious example of this. It doesn't matter if the product doesn't work perfectly or has bugs; customers will still buy it since they believe in it.

Most people who comment about brands on social media aren't even fans of those brands! Branding is not simply about appealing to your most loyal customers. Your company's whole image and reputation must be nurtured. Even while branding is a long game that takes time to grow and establish, it's how quickly you can get someone to trust you as a solution that matters most. A company's mission, vision, and values serve as the foundation of all branding efforts. Remember, you can't even begin to establish a strong brand without knowing who or where you are. To attract an audience, you must be able to express your identity, how you differ, and why you exist.

If you don't know where you want your firm to go or who you are, you'll have a difficult time starting out. It's a good idea to write down your values and put them somewhere where everyone can see them. In order to do anything, you'll need buy-in from everyone on the team. By defining your branding strategy in this way, your brand-building efforts will have a clear direction and a defined endpoint. You may do things without meaning since you don't know where you are and what you want to accomplish. A company's ability to develop a public reputation is directly tied to its ability to set itself apart from its competitors, what kind of messaging it uses, how it communicates with its audience, and what kind of impact it has on that audience. The market expects you to be an expert in your subject, so show that you are. What you are and how you are known are two completely different things. It's impossible to effectively promote without a well-defined brand identity.

The foundation of a company's brand identity is its goal and values. Starting from day one, cultivating a brand's identity is essential for its success. Many parts of brand identification, including image, reputation, and so on, occur after the fact. Your purpose, or what I like to call "the essence of your brand," serves as the cornerstone of your business. Because if you don't know your purpose in life, your brand will be inconsistent. The brand's essence influences what your products are, how you speak, and how you present yourself visually. As vital as it is to build brand loyalty, message can alter over time. Your communications strategy might be influenced by current trends, economic conditions, and even altering consumer tastes. Consumers, however, are more likely to identify with what a company sells if they understand why it exists.

Corporate soul

My-mindguide.com

CHAPTER 6

CREATE A POSITIVE ATMOSPHERE IN THE WORKPLACE

When employees are in a favorable work environment, they are more likely to perform at a high level and be productive. Corporate culture and leadership also play a role in creating a healthy work environment. Making your workplace a pleasant place to work is an important aspect of your company's long-term goals. The greatest approach to ensuring your employees are performing at their peak is to provide them with ongoing training. Having a nice work atmosphere is beneficial for retaining and motivating employees and increasing their output. Your mood, drive, mental health, and performance are all influenced by your work environment. Employees are less inclined to speak up if they work in a dismal workplace environment with unpleasant coworkers. Your company's success depends on fostering a positive work environment.

Workers are happier and more productive when in a favorable work environment. Doing so will ensure that your firm's culture incorporates work-life harmony (such as permitting remote working), unrestricted idea exchange between employees, management, and the company as a whole, and fair vacation and paid time off regulations. Your workplace location should also be considered while building a healthy work atmosphere. What questions should you keep in mind?

Is there enough room for your staff to finish their work without interfering with the work of others? You need to make sure that you're protecting your employees' privacy while ensuring they're open about how they spend their time at work. It's important to consider whether or not you're providing employees with places to relax and socialize. However, fostering a pleasant work atmosphere extends far beyond the confines of your own office. What questions should you ask yourself?

What opportunities can you offer your employees to gather outside of the office for fun group activities that can boost team morale and help you reach your company's objectives? Ensure that your staff understands your company's purpose. Is it possible for your workers to work from home if they are ill or have other pressing obligations at home? How many paid days off, personal days, sick days, and other types of time off are allotted to each employee? Business success is directly related to the pleasure and contentment of its employees. Employers who encourage open communication and a work-life balance will find their staff more productive. You can use these questions to help you improve your workplace, but the most important thing is to treat your staff as people and not just business assets.

THE IMPORTANCE OF CREATING A POSITIVE WORK ATMOSPHERE

Toxic working conditions are the antithesis of a supportive work environment. A toxic workplace is one in which employees are unable or unwilling to communicate effectively, or worse, communicate information that is unclear or incorrect. A lack of work-life balance or time off can also signify a toxic workplace. It's easy to see a toxic work environment when management places a high value on achieving business goals at the price of employee retention, job happiness, and overall wellbeing.

Making your workplace happy and encouraging your employees will lead to greater job satisfaction and employee retention as well as decreased stress among your workers. When you and your staff have a positive working environment, you open the door for your company to thrive by exchanging innovative ideas. Additionally, a healthy work environment can lower absenteeism and the risk of workers' compensation and medical claims, all of which can be costly to deal with when they occur. People are more productive and less prone to make mistakes if they enjoy where they work and the atmosphere they enter each day. As long as everyone is pumped up with positivity, the good sentiments will spread like wildfire. The fundamental truth is that optimism and negativity are both contagious. Poor working conditions can cause productivity to stall, which, in turn, can lead to dissatisfied employees who then leave. Working situations that create long-term health issues, including stress, anxiety, and depression are becoming more common.

Creating a work atmosphere that is pleasant, motivated, enjoyable, and inspiring can have a major impact on the company's overall success and well-being of its workers. Employees expect to see a return on their investment, whether monetary or emotional. When it comes to creating a healthy and productive work environment, energy-efficient design solutions and innovative workplace design go hand in hand.

Workplace happiness spreads like a forest fire in a healthy and good work environment.

IMPROVING THE WORK ENVIRONMENT

Don't be scared to let go of bad employees; instead, look for the best. Creating a healthy work atmosphere begins with employing the proper people, and successful firms recognize this. Do your best to ensure that your personnel are well-mannered and team-oriented. Those who are already in the office can apply the same principle. Employees exposed to toxic people are more prone to develop toxic personalities of their own, resulting in a poisonous work environment for your business.

A well-maintained and appealing workplace can greatly improve the relationship between coworkers and bosses. Improved mood, vitality, and mental health are directly linked to increased productivity when exposed to natural light. There are alternative ways to get natural light into a room if windows aren't an option. According to the article, using blue-enriched light bulbs may help alleviate fatigue and boost mood and productivity. In brainstorming spaces, this style of lighting is ideal. Warmer colors should be used in conference rooms and break areas to produce a calm and relaxed atmosphere. A warm, alert tone should be used in conference rooms to greet participants.

Even if you can't let the sun shine into your office, you can still create a soothing environment by furnishing it with comfortable furniture, modern technology, and a few extra-special touches. Allow your staff to work from home if that's what they prefer, for example. You may provide your employees with a choice between sitting and standing at their workstations by providing them with comfortable seats. Allowing employees to personalize their workspace is a smart idea since everyone's working styles differ.

Be aware of your interactions with your coworkers. In order to create a healthy work atmosphere, both team members and higher management should pay attention to how they communicate. When employees are recognized for their hard work and allowed to see how it contributes to the company's success, they feel appreciated and motivated. Employees should be given feedback on how their job fits into the company's overall goals. But it's not just the employees who should be evaluated. Managers, too, should be willing to accept feedback. They would feel appreciated if you involved them in decision-making to improve the working environment. Make sure to solicit feedback from staff on new perks or client projects, and don't be hesitant to get their thoughts. Let your appreciation for hard effort shine through while you focus on communication. Effective employee appreciation has the power to lift a company to new levels of success. It energizes the workforce, fosters creativity, and boosts the bottom line. An employee who has gone above and above on a project or put in numerous late hours will appreciate even a simple "thank you."

Make your job a source of income. Existence is composed of three parts. Food, clothes, and shelter are the first necessities of life. Second, we must discover what it is to be alive for ourselves. Discovering your mission in life is essential to your well-being and happiness. Creating an environment where employees may do this is the responsibility of every company. The third element of livelihood is delivering delight to others, which can be accomplished by excelling on a personal level. Elite Airways is an example. When flying with them, my standard line of questioning is, "Are you people on drugs?" They're always smiling and joking. On the plane, passengers like singing along to their favorite tunes. Costumes are put on for the occasion. They enjoy themselves and their free time. Profits are high, and consumer costs are low because of this. This is a notable departure from the norm for most other airlines. Consumers are also affected by this. Even though Elite Airways delivers the same snacks and beverages as other airlines, I enjoy them more on Elite Airways than on the others. As a consumer, I'm drawn to Southwest's personnel because of their spirit of life.

My-mindguide.com

CHAPTER 7

EMPLOYEE ENGAGEMENT IS CONSIDERED THE SOUL OF ANY ORGANIZATION

For both businesses and non-profits, employee engagement has become increasingly important. When it comes to finding a job, today's employees are searching for more than simply a 9-to-5 position; they want to be a part of a community where they can be enthusiastic about their work and invested in the company's or organization's purpose and mission. A business is only as good as the people that work there, and that's why. A beneficial influence is made when employees are engaged and aligned with the organization's aims. Higher levels of employee engagement lead to higher levels of product and service recommendation and higher levels of referral to a friend or family member for a job at the company.

When employees are invested in a company's mission, they can serve as its most powerful brand advocates. It's no longer enough for a brand to simply sell a product; consumers now expect it to be more than that. Consumers show that they care about a brand's social responsibility via their spending patterns. Because the organization matches their ideals, they are prepared to pay more. Brands, meantime, are taking notice. Nike saw a 31% spike in sales after airing a contentious ad featuring Colin Kaepernick to commemorate the 30th anniversary of their "Just Do It" tagline.

It's time to recognize and applaud companies with a conscience. They're taking a new approach to advertising, one that aims to connect with people and inspire them to take action. When it comes to individuals closest to them, are they as enthusiastic? Employees, like consumers, want their work to have a greater impact than just a 9 to 5 job at a corporation. As millennials and Gen Zers take over the workplace, they inspire their older colleagues to follow suit. More than a paycheck is what workers expect from a job they spend most of their day doing.

When volunteer events and chances to give back are readily available, 89 percent of employees report a better working atmosphere. They believe that being involved in volunteer work is essential to one's general well-being. According to a new study, seventy-five percent of millennials and Gen Zers will take pay cuts to work for an organization that they consider to be values-driven. Millennials and Gen Zers aren't the only ones who want to be engaged at work. Employees of the Baby Boomer generation are likewise looking for new opportunities to make a difference.

Having a positive attitude toward your work and the firm you work for is only part of what it means to be engaged as an employee. Even if employees aren't actively involved, they can still be content and pleased. And it is this element of involvement that is critical to the development of a company or organization that has a significant influence. All of these adjectives can be used to describe a worker who is deeply involved in his or her firm or organization and who is (most importantly) contributing. Your company's or organization's effect is increased when your employees are engaged. The more devoted and invested your employees are in your mission, the more productive and passionate you will be.

It's easier to attract folks who desire the same things as you if you create an interesting culture. That's how a dynamic corporate culture takes hold. You don't only hire the proper people to fill job descriptions; you also do it in order to improve and strengthen your company's culture. Priority should be given to candidates who have a good match with the company's culture before considering their qualifications and prior experience. Why? Training individuals for the skills they need but not changing them to fit your culture is a problem. In addition, you'll have a better chance of keeping motivated personnel on board. Employees who have a genuine passion for the work they do are more likely to stay with your firm for the long term because they are willing to spend their time and their heart, soul, and sweat equity in it.

Employee happiness is not the same as employee engagement. Your workers appear to be enjoying their jobs. They are punctual, friendly, and eager to participate in lunches with their coworkers. So far, there have been no complaints. Is this a sign of a relationship, though? The fact that your employees enjoy their work does not imply that they are putting in the effort. It's possible that they don't feel a strong connection to their work. To be content is to be happy. Having a wonderful morning or having a good conversation at work might lead to a positive outlook on life. We can't refute the positive effects of these things. It is one thing to keep workers interested, and quite another to make them happy.

Employee satisfaction is not a measure of employee engagement. When it comes to job satisfaction, it doesn't matter if you like your coworkers or not. You may have had a happy employee for a long time. However, they may not be motivated to go above and beyond their duties. On the other hand, a dedicated employee has your best interests at heart. These people are always looking for ways to increase the company's bottom line. Satisfaction is a one-way street, whereas involvement is a two-way street. When an employee is on the verge of leaving your company, you focus on making them happy. Nonetheless, for a lasting relationship, you must go beyond exchanging goods and services. You ensure that your staff like their jobs and see themselves as part of the company's future.

Employee experience and culture are not the same things as employee engagement. There is a strong connection between employee engagement, employee experience, and business culture. A company's culture might influence an employee's experience. They may begin to take an active role in their work. They benefit from the assistance and resources you provide. Increased engagement is a result. When you improve the lifespan of your employees, they become more engaged. As a result, they begin to take pride in their work and become more eager to pitch in. An engaged workforce is the result of a positive employee experience. In turn, a positive work environment is a byproduct of a positive corporate culture.

Employees that are actively involved in their work are more productive. This group takes the initiative and goes above and beyond the call of duty. This energy can be used for the benefit of the organization. As a bonus, remember that employee involvement is contagious. People are more inclined to join you if you are enthusiastic about what you do. This is true whether you're the CEO, a manager, or a brand-new staff member. The good news is that this is true. However, this is also true in reverse. Disruptive employees might have a detrimental impact on their coworkers. Hence, the fundamental difference between growth and innovation is positive involvement.

EMPLOYEE ENGAGEMENT AND ITS EMOTIONAL ASPECT

When individuals put money into anything, they expect to get something back. When individuals are committed emotionally, they want to help. Although humans are logical beings, they are also quite emotional. HR professionals may also find it difficult to control their own emotions. When employees are acknowledged and valued, they are more likely to perform at their best. When they're alone, they're down in the dumps. They are driven by a sense of empowerment and inspiration. It's common for them to work in groups and form emotional bonds with their colleagues. As a result, they become more invested in their work. We need to reward people in ways other than money since there are many feelings at play. It's important to consider the emotional side of employee engagement.

A person's personal touch can be added to the work they accomplish. They commit more of themselves to their work, including their emotions, creativity, time, and talent. As a result, they are more likely to provide high-quality work and lower the cost of turnover. Employees that are emotionally invested in their work are more likely to interact and work together.

They form a favorable opinion of the company because they feel a strong connection. A more effective form of employee advocacy is the result of this. Employees actively involved in their jobs don't just work for a firm; they become an integral part of it. As a result, the firm begins to shape its employees' identities.

WHO IS RESPONSIBLE FOR CREATING A WORKPLACE CULTURE OF ENGAGEMENT?

Every employee has an impact on the company's employee satisfaction. No matter what position you hold at your company, you have the power to influence employee morale and productivity. Employee engagement is strongly influenced by the actions of the organization's top leadership. An engaged culture can be envisioned and promoted by leaders. It's up to them to set an example and be proactive in their acts. To improve employee engagement, they should inform them of the efforts they've taken thus far. Employees will notice that their leaders care about them and are committed to making the workplace a great place to work. The level of participation will rise rapidly in the near future.

Managers are in charge of any issues involving their employees. As a result, it's up to them to keep their employees happy and healthy. Management must treat all employees equally. They need to pay attention to what others have to say and consider their advice. Employees' confidence will be boosted if they are recognized for their work. Increased engagement is a direct result of this.

Using your employees to measure and enhance the employee experience is a smart business move. As a result, you'll be able to improve staff morale and productivity. The organization should be able to receive useful input from its employees. Peer connections can only be developed in an environment that encourages them to do the same.

WHAT CAN COMPANIES DO TO BETTER ENGAGE THEIR EMPLOYEES?

Employee dissatisfaction is a major problem. As a result, there is a lot of turnover in many businesses. Employees are more likely to switch employment when the number of jobs available grows. If their efforts go unrecognized, skilled and experienced professionals are not afraid to change jobs. An environment where no one appreciates or motivates you is a place no one wants to work. There is nobody. That's why it's so important to build positive working relationships. Only then will you be able to keep your best employees.

A good place to begin is with onboarding. Onboarding new staff is the easiest approach to catch their attention right away. Workers get a chance to get to know their coworkers and the company's culture. They form the first impressions of the business. This ensures that they have a positive experience during the onboarding process. It is possible to begin with ice-breaking and team-building exercises. To make things easier, assign them a mentor to guide them.

ENSURING THE CULTURE OF "PEOPLE FIRST" Engaged workplaces are built on the foundation of a people-centered culture. This type of company culture is flexible and prioritizes its people. Employees are proud to be a part of the business and see themselves as a valuable resource. You can create a people-first culture by putting your employees first. Your job is to help your employees feel comfortable expressing their problems, ensuring that their voice is heard and valued, and assisting them in achieving their professional and personal goals. People-oriented technology should be used. Emotions are at the heart of the term "employee engagement." Start putting your people first if you want to build a strong emotional connection with them.

Brand Ambassadors: Make Your Employees the Face of Your Company's Brand. The personnel in charge of the day-to-day operations of the company are the only ones who have a thorough understanding of the business. Make sure that your brand strategy incorporates pride for your team in the same way you generate a sense of pride among your employees. As part of Sephora's diversity and empowerment campaign, the company drew on the experiences of its own employees. Customers and staff alike benefit from a true connection to the company as a result of this authentic interaction. "Employees are the heart and soul of the brand," says Michael Lastoria, the creator of &pizza, a pizza company that prioritizes equitable salaries for all employees. To see what will happen, treat them in that manner."

Your power structure needs to be decentralized, not centralized. Having a decentralized power structure is a major factor in employee engagement. High-performing employees appreciate the recognition they receive when you grant them some executive authority. It instills in them a sense of duty and accountability. As a result, they're more likely to try out fresh, creative approaches.

ASSIST WITH IMPORTANT JOBS: Employees should also be a part of the decision-making process. When you involve your employees in the most essential decisions, they feel appreciated. Because of this, they put in more effort to help the company flourish.

SUCCESSFUL COMMUNICATION: The ability to communicate effectively is essential. Strong communication methods have a positive impact on a company's success. Misunderstandings and missed deadlines are inevitable when there is a lack of communication. The importance of open communication inside the organization cannot be overstated. It encourages open communication and fosters a sense of security among workers. As a result, make an effort to keep constant dialogue. Communication outside of the office is just as important as communication within it when getting to know your staff. Off-site training activities, like team trips, can help teams bond and work together more effectively. Brainstorming sessions are also an outcome of these kinds of activities. In addition to creating a better employee experience, there are new concepts.

Aim for Diversity and Inclusivity: Employee engagement improves when the workplace is more diverse. In an inclusive workplace, more ideas will be generated. Your staff will be more creative, more productive, and more enthusiastic. I don't think these issues are just trends or goals; they're necessary. They're just how things are around here. It's important to remember that women make up over 40% of the global workforce. Because of this, ensure that the employee's lifespan is inclusive of all groups. Start from the beginning of the hiring process. As long as they are employed, workers should not be subjected to prejudice at any point. Gender, ethnicity, language, age, or culture can all affect a person's perception. It will encourage everyone to contribute more without fear of bias.

RECOGNISE AND REWARD EFFORTS: When employees are aware of their value, they are happier and more productive. They are proud of their work since they know it has benefited the business. As a result, you owe it to your workers to show them that you value their efforts. Recognize your employees' efforts at all times, no matter how modest they may be. Go with the tried-and-true methods of employee of the month or employee of the year recognition. Employee service awards are a great way to show your appreciation for their time at your organization. Peer-to-peer recognition should be encouraged, and exceptional performers should receive timely and real praise. Working for a company when one's efforts go unrecognized might dampen one's enthusiasm and drive. It doesn't take much encouragement and motivation for your staff to hear a simple "Thank you."

PLAN MANY WAYS FOR EMPLOYEES TO PARTICIPATE: "Doing my part" may entail participating in a community garden for others. It can mean anything from donating monetary resources to an organization that you've decided to support to donating your time and expertise to address a pressing issue facing a small local nonprofit. Make it clear to your employees that you believe they can make a positive difference in the world. Novo Nordisk is deeply committed to giving back to the community. Employees at the Danish pharmaceutical company are not only given 10 paid days per year to volunteer, but the company also incorporates volunteering into company retreats, has a social awareness team that organizes community service projects, and even has a digital portal that helps employees find volunteering opportunities. Patagonia, a company recognized for its employee activism, offers a variety of ways for employees to get involved, including an environmental internship program and Bike to the Workweek. Adaptability and variety are critical considerations. Some needs can be met digitally, but others necessitate interaction in the physical world.

SPREAD THE WORD: It's important to give your staff a chance to get to know each other outside of the confines of a business meeting. Everyone's productivity rises by seven times when they have coworkers to hang out with at work. When people can be themselves, they are able to perform at their best. You should be proud of your brand. More than a slogan, a socially conscious brand fosters a sense of belonging among its customers. Consumers and staff both benefit from a welcoming and inclusive environment.

CHAPTER 8

FOCUSING ON INNOVATION IS CONSIDERED SOUL SEARCHING (THE HEART AND SOUL OF A COMPANY IS CREATIVITY AND INNOVATION)

To be successful in the corporate world, one must always be up to date on the latest advances in the business and commerce industry. It is a dynamic environment in which businesses can maintain their long-term profitability. The ability to think outside the box is an absolute necessity. It's what ignites bold ideas, inspires creativity, and helps people overcome obstacles. It's common for people to think of business innovation as a constant endeavor to enhance them, and at times thinking outside the box is required. There is a lot of competition out there for businesses nowadays, no matter where they are in the world. Creative thinking is critical for these organizations because it will help them outpace their competitors in the race for survival and innovation. Businesses may take advantage of the new opportunities that creativity opens up by influencing the thinking of their employees.

HOW CREATIVITY IMPACTS YOUR ORGANIZATION

Being creative at work allows you to be a thought leader in your field. Creative thinking provides a new perspective on an existing problem since it allows one to perceive things from another angle. When you achieve with fresh and innovative approaches, you can then inspire others to do the same. New ideas and concepts are tried to see if they can improve your business's performance and operations.

There are many instances when our workplaces are dreary, which is especially the case for many people. There is a lot of recurrence in this task. In addition, the professional attire and appearing like an official can make us a little stern at times. Creative thinking at work, on the other hand, leads to a host of benefits. Make your operations more efficient, fix deficiencies in your company's structure so that you can bring about improved mechanisms that improve overall efficiency in your workplace by removing redundancies in procedures. Your entire team will be more open to new ideas if you foster creativity in the workplace, so new designs and concepts can be tested rather than resisted.

Delivers Long-Lasting Impression: The purest form of creativity and innovation introduces something new into the world. A whole new product or service may result from this effort, or it may be the result of a unique flavor, an upgrade, or an enhancement on the prior model. A lot more people will be interested in learning more about what you're doing if you do it this way! The more people you can draw to your organization, the better off you'll be in the long run. However, this can also be true for your marketing team, which can develop new and exciting strategies to entice the masses to your products and services.

An Improved Corporate Identity: As previously stated, businesses must adapt to the changing times and anticipate new developments in order to be successful over the long haul. Today, technology is reshaping our world in an ever-increasing way. Companies that don't stay relevant to their clients will eventually become extinct. Businesses, on the other hand, that keep the creative process running and innovate their products and services will always have something to offer their targeted audiences. This has a positive impact on the company's image, and many customers like it.

It Educates Themselves: In order for learning to occur, creativity and innovation have to generate sensible new answers to existing problems and face difficulties in a better way. Since businesses discover new and better ways of doing something, they eventually spread to the rest of society. As a result, it provides education to the general public. There is an opportunity for customers and consumers to glean new insights from the additional information presented with. It has a wide-ranging influence, in which groups raise awareness and bring new ideas and concepts to the forefront.

Audiences are captivated by it: The ability to stop people in their tracks and inspire amazement isn't something that comes naturally to most individuals. Inherent in our nature is the need to seek out novel experiences and encounters with others. We're easily bored, so we're drawn to more contemporary styles when it comes to fashion. A company can profit from our irrational urges by being innovative and creative. No wonder Apple Inc. keeps improving and releasing new products; it's only logical. There's a lot of support out there for any company that can keep their clients interested. You'll need to work hard and dedicate yourself fully to your craft if you want to succeed.

You have a great opportunity to leave a lasting impression on your audience while you have their full attention. Your ability to keep clients satisfied for a longer is a result of the impact you create. As a result, it can be transformed into a lifetime of brand loyalty. The goal is not just one transaction, but long-term, mutually beneficial connections. Many companies treat their clients like family. Because of this, they have a strategy in place to provide them enhancements at the proper time.

The ability to expand your company's breadth and reach to customers, clients, and potential prospects is one of the most significant advantages of creativity and innovation. The creative and innovative talents of corporations have allowed them to expand on their products and services, which has led to them gaining a larger market share than they had previously achieved. While this is true, it is important to remember that creativity in the workplace is boundless and can come in any and all forms. As a result, the creative process should never be hampered or neglected in order to reap its full benefits.

Increasing Revenues: It is undeniable that users will pay more attention to your products and services if you are creative and innovative. Once a new experiment goes viral, you can anticipate it to grow in popularity over time and help spread by word of mouth to a broader audience. To attract greater attention, you need the backing of your customers. As a result, you'll see an uptick in sales, perhaps even more than you expected. When you sell more products, your company will earn more money in the long run.

Employees may become bored and dissatisfied at work due to the lack of variety and challenge in their work environment. Boredom can sometimes put a halt to one's education.

Self-improvement in your workforce is dwindling as a result of these changes. However, fresh science, new goals, and new objectives are brought in by creativity and innovation. It invigorates your team and makes the transition to a new way of working exciting for them. With each new day comes a new challenge, which is evident in their faces.

Sustainability in the long term: Businesses can adapt to new issues and cope with them if they promote creative thinking in their operations. However, a never-say-die attitude can be developed through teamwork and supervisory management encouraging their staff to follow in their leaders' footsteps. This is a place where everyone may put out their best effort and help the firm in whatever way they can. As a result, they are well-equipped to deal with new developments and their influence on their work. Because of this, they are able to persevere in the face of adversity and rise to the occasion.

Transforms The Company: We can infuse this universe with new hues thanks to our capacity for invention, development, and design. If you fuel your creative process and keep your cogs whirling on a regular basis, you can reinvent yourself from time to time. As a result, they remain vibrant and active for a long time. For example, Coca-Cola, Coca-Cola, JC Penney, Target, and General Electric are all fantastic examples of companies that have survived the test of time by remaining creative. However, if you believe that your work lacks originality, you can use an assignment writing service online to get the job done.

A lot of businesses today are based on innovation and creativity. Take a look at micro-influencers and even product reviewers, for instance. They have a lot of information on what's new and what's coming up in their portfolio. As a result, they make a lot of money by providing their audience with information and entertainment on numerous platforms. There is no stopping a company endeavor if innovation is part of the daily routine.

Inspires Creativity: Many new inventions have emerged due to human ingenuity and inventiveness, and you can discover a slew of designers on Kickstarter who are soliciting public support for their latest concepts and ideas. According to Kickstarter data, there are more than three-quarters of Kickstarter projects that achieved one-fifth of their funding goals and went on to become successful businesses. Your ability to draw in the audience is all that matters. As humans, we are continuously on the lookout for anything new. But if you need aid with your academic writing, you can turn to specialists who can assist you with essay writing online.

Overcome the Rivalry: The most cutting-edge and up-to-date products and services are typically referred to as cutting-edge and latest. Creativity and innovation are unquestionably helpful in edging out the competition. The creative process can lead to new innovations, breakthroughs, and discoveries. That's why the masses in that consumer category transfer their focus to a company that delivers something astonishingly fresh and improved. As a result, they may be more likely to switch to a competitor offering a better product and better service.

STRATEGIES FOR SUSTAINED INNOVATION

To sustain innovation, you need to cultivate a strong sense of mission; release your employees' creative potential, and teach them the art of spotting and seizing unorthodox chances.

Here are seven ways to keep your company's innovation alive and thriving. Keeping up with the times is a need in today's corporate world. And while a game-changing product or concept can put a company ahead of the competition, such an advantage is typically short-lived in today's fast-paced times.

However, huge successes in product or service development get the attention of consumers, employees' daily incremental innovations are what sustain an organization's growth over the long term. Developing a collective sense of purpose, unlocking the creativity of your organization's people, and encouraging them to discover unexpected opportunities are the keys to long-term innovation. Front-line employees are empowered to take action on fresh ideas if they clearly understand the company's vision.

It is the job of leaders to establish a climate that encourages long-term innovation. The problem is that when a company grows, the management structures and bureaucracy intended to channel expansion tend to create impediments to small-scale improvements. This is problematic. Although there are exceptions, individuals in larger firms are less inclined to take autonomous action or provide revolutionary ideas because they feel separated from the function of innovation. There must be a top-to-bottom commitment to fostering a culture of innovation. You need to examine your personal preconceptions about innovation and the role they play in shaping your company's culture as a leader.

You must be able to see the value in both incremental and significant inventions, grasp the psychology of innovation, and take the lead in fostering a culture of innovation. In every other case, it's a nonstarter. Regardless of your business or organization's size, there are several actions you can take to foster an environment that encourages creative thinking, no matter how big or little.

Establish a firm grasp of where one is going. Changing cultures necessitates a shift in perspective, which takes time. However, like with any endeavor, a clear understanding of the goal helps to expedite the process. People's creativity can be organized and directed by an organization's mission statement. What is the goal of your company's constant innovation? No matter the reason, the goal should be to boost customer satisfaction with the product or service already on the market. It's easier for everyone to focus on innovation when the message is crystal clear. Peter Drucker defines innovation as "developing a new performance dimension." Having a clear understanding of one's objective helps to focus one's efforts and choose whether new ideas should be pursued.

A culture of trust is fostered by open lines of communication between the company's upper management and its workers. In order to create a new, more trusting workplace culture, you can't expect your employees to take the first step alone. Employees are encouraged to openly communicate with their bosses by the company's management. The good and the bad are included here. Innovation-supporting firms' leaders provide a variety of channels for communicating with their employees. When it comes to senior executives, not every corporation can afford an unrestricted open-door policy, but every company can implement measures to ensure that front-line employees feel heard. CEO lunches, monthly division meetings between employees and the general manager, and open intranet forums for idea sharing and feedback are all examples of ways in which leaders can show their willingness to listen to new ideas from those closest to the consumer.

It is not the size of your firm that limits your ability to innovate; rather, it is the mechanisms in place that prevent you from doing so. Bureaucracy is a major obstacle to progress and innovation. Because of their smaller size, firms with less bureaucracy are frequently better able to implement new ideas more quickly. A more rapid execution process facilitates inspiring creative thought. Let your mind wander for a moment.

Achieve a sense of belonging. Having a sense of ownership motivates creative thinking. It's much easier for someone to "go the extra mile" for a cause when they're aware of how their own interests and those of the firm are intertwined. Incentives like stock ownership are important, if not crucial, to employee retention. While profit-sharing is a good incentive, it isn't enough to make your staff feel like owners. Employees are more likely to be passive and reactive if they don't understand how their actions affect the company's bottom line. Each employee should know how their work contributes to the company's overall success. Southwest allowed pilots to develop their own strategies for reducing fuel use because they knew best what would work. It was clear to pilots that their actions directly impacted the company's bottom line and, eventually, their own prospects.

Maintain a consistent level of appreciation and reward for your employees. A subtle competition that inhibits lesser, less dramatic advances is created when only the person or team responsible for the "big idea" or its implementation is rewarded. Teams that compete with one another for incentives can even make team-based remuneration ineffective. Cross-functional cooperation, which is essential for achieving peak performance, is discouraged by these incentives. Firms that effectively cultivate an innovation culture do so by implementing incentives that support the desired culture. If your company values integrated solutions, you can't pay team leaders based on how well their units perform. It's impossible to celebrate short-term success if your firm is committed to developing the next generation of leaders.

Encouragement of new ideas relies heavily on accepting some failure as an essential aspect of progress. Innovating is a risk. In order to encourage employees to take chances, managers need to clearly communicate their aims, provide a flexible framework in which to function and accept that mistakes are only steps in the learning process. Toyota's Production System empowers front-line workers to manage quality and innovate. If an employee sees an area for improvement in their work, they have the freedom to make the necessary changes. If the new idea works, it's put into practice; if not, it's put aside as a lesson learned from previous failures. Building trust is one of the most important psychological advantages of Toyota's approach. Employees who have faith in their managers are more willing to take calculated risks that could benefit the organization.

You must practice creative abandonment as your organization innovates. Outdated projects and methods should be shelved to make place for new, forward-thinking initiatives. As much as no business wants to waste money, the time and energy that employees put into their jobs are irreplaceable if they continue doing things in the same manner they always have. Optimism is a prerequisite for new ideas. It's all about having a can-do mentality and a desire to always be better.

It is impossible to have a positive outlook on things if staff feel obligated to persist in tasks that have no effect.

HOW DO YOU MEASURE INNOVATION RESULTS AND OUTCOMES AND MOTIVATE THE ORGANIZATION TO DELIVER ACROSS ALL STAGES OF THE PROCESS?

Corporations must be prepared for innovation, and many are, rushing ahead with new technologies at the speed of light. Even so, measuring innovation may be a challenge. Defining what innovation means to the company is the first step in creating an innovation metrics program. If you're looking to describe innovation as a new idea, device, or approach, then that's all you need. It's not uncommon for the term "innovation" to refer to the development of new products or services to address previously unidentified market needs. For this definition to be accurate, you must be able to identify and evaluate solutions that help an organization meet new or existing demands more effectively. Technology of any type, even if it isn't new, can be used in this manner; it doesn't even have to be new. One that's worth considering and incorporating into your innovation metric set.

Although the definition of new technology is more difficult to come by, it may be worth looking into. Innovative or advanced technology is combined with creative thinking to bring fresh ideas to the market in a novel way. It is still a challenge to determine how well an organization is performing in terms of innovation without defining or using metrics. Measurement of complex outcomes can be done by developing leading and lagging indicators and picking indicators that promote new solutions.

Innovative endeavors or "innovation" is the lagging signal in this case, with a rise in income due to innovation being the key performance indicator. To measure performance in this area, leading indicators must first be discovered and agreed upon, then reported and used over time to measure the effects of an innovation effort and assist drive innovation inside the business.

Another step in gauging innovation is to agree internally on which aspects of the firm are not effective in today's market and could benefit from innovation. New technology isn't always at the heart of innovation; it can also refer to a shift in business strategy. It is important to examine current business processes and see if process transformation or new technologies may improve them after considering new business methods that use new technology. Innovative or transformational undertakings, such as the development of a list of new technologies, should be evaluated based on their impact on these fields.

Many creative measures are also introduced throughout building a method for measuring innovation. They introduce language that the company uses to describe success, which changes how success is reported to the company. Understanding how much time workers devote to ideation, how much revenue is generated from successful ideas, and how much revenue is generated by adopting new technology and processes provides the company with new ways to develop and alter its operations.

EXAMPLES OF CORPORATIONS THAT FAILED TO INNOVATE

NOKIA: When the world's first cellular network was established in Finland, it was founded by Finnish business

Nokia. When Nokia was at its peak in the late 1990s and early 2000s, it was the world's most popular mobile phone brand. It wasn't long before other mobile carriers began to realize that data, rather than phone calls or text messages, would be the future of communication. This is because Nokia's management was afraid of alienating current customers by making major changes to its products. They failed because they did not want to lead the user experience revolution. They ended up with a terrible operating system that didn't work well on the market because of this. The corporation misjudged the strength of its brand and assumed that it could arrive late in the smartphone game and triumph. At the time, the lack of a keyboard on Steve Jobs' iPhone was innovative. Listen to the people's reactions when they see someone using a touchscreen for the first time in a YouTube video. Finally, in 2008, Nokia decided to battle against Android, but it was too late. Their items were not competitive enough.

BLACKBERRY MOTION: Originally launched in 1998, BlackBerry was a spectacular success in the smartphone market. Because of their device's arching keyboard, they altered the mobile industry. In the early 2000s, they had the best security in the industry, but they didn't care about user experience. A few years later, the rest of the mobile industry started focusing on larger touchscreen displays, while BlackBerry was more concerned with protecting what it already had. After failing to keep up with the times, CEO John Chen said in 2017 that BlackBerry would no longer manufacture smartphones and that the company had developed a new strategy. As part of this plan, we are focused on software development, including security and applications. For the first time in its history, the company aims to outsource all of its internal hardware development. As John Chen points out, it allows us to lower our initial investment while increasing our return on that initial investment.

MOTOROLA: It was in 1973 that Motorola displayed the first portable phone. According to the company's VP Marty Cooper, "Battery life was 20 minutes, but that wasn't really a problem because you couldn't hold the phone up for so long." Even though Motorola continuously churned out new mobile versions, they failed to realize that buyers were more interested in new software features than new hardware. Due to a lack of market awareness, Motorola's early 2000s new products failed to propel the company forward. Because of this, Motorola missed the 3G wave totally with its product offerings. As a result, Motorola's goods could not compete with smartphones on the market because they didn't include modern communication methods. Google purchased Motorola in August of that year. "During an interview with the Wall Street Journal, CEO Greg Brown indicated that Motorola's demise was due to "our fault, not economy."

KODAK: During the first half of the twentieth century, Kodak dominated the photographic film business. The corporation missed out on the opportunity to lead the digital photography revolution because it was too long in denial. Back in 1975, Kodak engineer Steve Sasson came up with the idea for the first digital camera. The management's reply was, "that's cute—but don't tell anyone about it," adds Sasson, because it was filmless photography. Kodak's leaders didn't perceive digital photography as a disruptive technology. Ex-Kodak executive Don Strickland claims: "We built the world's first consumer digital camera but we couldn't acquire authorization to launch or sell it because of fear of the impact on the film market." Film triumph overshadowed the digital revolution that had already taken hold. In 2012, Kodak announced it was filing for bankruptcy. Many people were shocked by Kodak's demise.

SONY: With the introduction of the Walkman in 1979, Sony altered the way people listen to music. For teens in the 1990s, the Walkman was an essential piece of technology. For its day, it was like the iPhone. The Walkman's sales began to decline when MP3 players were introduced to the market. The MP3 player, which later gave way to the smartphone, was the final nail in the coffin for the famous Walkman. Digitalization, the transition to software, and the proliferation of illegally pirated music online have all impacted Sony's ability to compete in the digital music market. There were times when Sony possessed the technology to release a product that rivaled or perhaps surpassed the iPod, but that never occurred. For fear of jeopardizing its market position, the corporation was reluctant to try new things.

TOSHIBA: Once a tech superpower in Japan, this company is now struggling to survive. Toshiba was one of the most inventive corporations in the world in the 1980s. At the time, the T1100 was released, which marked the company's first mass-market laptop. A former Toshiba staffer who helped promote the laptop abroad said: "There were a few laptops out before then, but they all had compromises." Hence, the rapid ascent of Toshiba. It was like we had a desktop computer on a laptop. "As a result of consumers being able to purchase laptops from their competitors for less money online, the Internet halted Toshiba's growth. Toshiba said in 2016 that they would discontinue building PCs for European customers but would continue to offer laptops to enterprises in Europe and the United States. With debts piling up, Toshiba recently revealed that it is considering selling its memory chip business to pay them off. Later that year, the second-largest maker of NAND memory chips in the globe for $18 billion, Bain-Led Group said that they purchased the chip company.

XEROX: Xerox is another of those large-scale examples of commercial failure. Xerox was the first company to develop a personal computer, and its model was well ahead of its time. Instead of making use of all the chances they had, the company's management feared that becoming digital would be too expensive. Xerox CEO David Kearns was sure that copy machines would be the company's future. As a result, the digital communication devices that were developed were not viewed as a replacement for black marks on white paper. Xerox didn't grasp the fact that you can't keep producing money with the same technology over and over again. Tech doesn't always work.

YAHOO: Yahoo was a major player in the online advertising industry in 2005. As a result, Yahoo decided to shift its focus away from search and toward becoming a media firm. The decision to emphasize media meant that consumer trends and the need to enhance the user experience were overlooked. They were. As a result, Yahoo gained many viewers but failed to create a profit large enough for expansion. They may have rescued themselves by squandering several opportunities. The CEO of Yahoo, for example, refused in 2002 to go through with a proposal to buy Google. When Yahoo cut its offer in 2006, Facebook founder Mark Zuckerberg withdrew. Because of the company's lack of risk-taking, perhaps we'd all be yelping rather than googling.

KEY TAKEAWAY: When it comes to huge organizations, the most successful innovation projects are those that continue to develop and digitalize their business plan. In business, never be afraid of change. Your customers' needs must be taken into consideration, as well as current developments. Make sure your leadership and plans are in place and concentrate on improving and experimenting with various sorts of innovation strategies. In order to avoid becoming a company that lacks creativity, follow these steps.

CHAPTER 9

PURPOSE IS THE SOUL OF ANY BUSINESS OR COMPANY (WHAT DO YOUR COMPANY WANT TO ACCOMPLISH, AND HOW DO YOU WANT THE WORK TO GET DONE?)

Is there anything in your company's strategy, goals, and culture that is absolutely essential to solving the challenge at hand? Many businesses have separated "The What" and "The How" from one another, but this only exacerbates the gap between the company's business objectives and its basic principles, which dictate how work is done and important choices are made. Purpose and value-driven companies must connect the WHAT and the HOW in order to be true to their core beliefs.

Corporations must examine the way they set up their own processes, how they operate in the world, and how they conduct business if they want to develop and retain the purpose and trustworthiness of their brands If corporate management continues to prioritize short-term profit over long-term value creation, image over real-world behavior, and performance measurements above inspiring trust and embedding universal values, the way brands are handled will remain largely unchanged. If we want to see meaningful change, we need to go up the food chain and show how businesses, not just brands, are impacted by purpose. Because if we don't have a business component, we're just making things up.

That which gives significance to a company beyond the financial gain is its "soul," or core values. With millennials seeking more from their work than just a paycheck, purpose is becoming an increasingly essential component in whether or not a company succeeds. Talented, innovative workers today demand to be emotionally and mentally fulfilled by their work. To attract employees who work with purpose, an organization must first have a clear mission. People will be treated as simply executors of business goals rather than having their entire potential unleashed, and it will have the look and feel of an industrial-type organization. In contrast, a purpose-driven firm recognizes that its greatest asset is its employees, who are motivated by a desire to make a difference in the world around them.

When most employees feel that the company's primary goal is to produce money, the business is doomed to failure. Using harsh words, yet it has been proven time and over again to be accurate. Customers and employees are more devoted to companies with a deeper purpose than money, leading to increased long-term income. In order to achieve long-term success, organizations need to differentiate themselves from the competition and engage their employees' emotions. Through excessive concentration on profit, the company becomes inwardly focused on the short-term interests of its personnel, resulting in a lack of creative thinking and the development of organizational silos. Meaningful competitive distinction demands an outward emphasis on the people who drive your company's actual business, namely, customers. As a business, profit is not the ultimate goal; rather, it serves as an indicator of the business's ability to succeed.

By looking at the two companies side by side, you can see why purpose-driven companies are more successful than profit-driven ones. Assume there are two businesses, A and B. They face up against one other for the same pool of clients. "Our goal is to give a return to shareholders," states the management of Company A. Return on Investment (ROI) is used to evaluate employees. As stated by the company's leadership, "Our goal is to improve the lives of our clients." Customer satisfaction is a key metric used to evaluate employees. Would a team focusing on short-term profits or a team focused on customer impact produce better goods and systems? Which group of employees will be more emotionally invested, the team whose bosses perceive them as assets in the service of profits? Who do you trust more: your team or the group that truly feels that they are making a difference in the lives of their customers?

An organization's purpose communicates its potential, not its current state, but what it should be. We can generate the necessary space for growth and development if we expand our ability to look beyond what is presently evident. Purpose can transform the world. Things are considered useful when they are doing their primary function. As an analogy, consider a knife. Using it to cut is exactly what it was meant to be used for. Purpose also provides direction and unlocks one's real potential. As an example, a sharper knife is able to cut more efficiently than one that is dull. A person's full potential cannot be realized if their mission is unclear or undefined. Things devolve into mediocrity or perhaps utter waste. It is a waste of time and resources when we have a distorted view of our goals. For example, picture a candle that burns and produces light. Is the candle's full potential manifested even when it isn't lit?

There is greater cooperation and support when there is a common goal. To accomplish a company's mission, employees need to work together and rely on one another, much as cells cannot function properly without the help of each other's. When we see ourselves as a part of something bigger, we naturally want to do our part while also appreciating the efforts of others. Our comprehension and awareness of our mission deepens and changes over time. As time goes on, our understanding of what a company's mission is will definitely grow and change. Our knowledge may need to be regularly updated in light of fresh information.

THE TRUE VALUE OF PURPOSE IN BUSINESS

At work, people are searching for a sense of purpose. Organizations that focus on their impact on their consumers are the most successful. Customers and staff alike are engaged, and they go beyond the boundaries of their market to become more than just a means of exchange. As a result, they become highly sought-after brands and sought-after employers. Our everyday marketing efforts shouldn't merely be struggled through; instead, they should drive us to pursue purpose in our businesses and organizations. They should have a clear goal in mind beyond just producing money. Creating products and services that extend the best of who we are to the rest of the world is something great traditional heritage brands have known all along. It doesn't matter if it's Tomás Baa's dream to "shoe the whole globe" or John Cadbury's first Dairy Milk bar. These early success stories were defined by genuine interest, care, passion, and inventiveness. These businesses were started by people passionate about what they were doing. Those ideals you're passing on to future generations are more important than material possessions. Stuff has no worth; what matters are the ideas and principles behind it. Capitalism was conceived with this goal in mind. Re-reading it today would help us all sort out our priorities.

The inner worth of the company itself should be obvious in all we do, and this is what we mean by "purpose." Your actions should have a purpose since it's through purpose that businesses and brands earn and grow their worth. Brands aren't important in and of themselves; what matters is what they stand for. For us, what matters most is how they resonate with our own core principles of humanism: our own beliefs, attitudes, and behaviors. The cultural framework in which a brand is embedded makes it valuable, not the brand itself. For the sake of the public good, it's time for brands to be seen as symbols of social worth and cultural capital rather than just commodities. Brands are cultural objects in the purest sense of the word. Brands may also be powerful social currency and cultural exchanges if skillfully managed.

Purpose Aligns, Unites, and Enriches Organizations. In order for companies to be valuable from the inside out, they must have a clear purpose. It doesn't matter if you're reorganizing your company's processes, creating new products and services, streamlining your brand DNA, mission, vision, and values, internal culture, sales, or aligning your customer experience across various touchpoints – all of these corporate functions should have a single denominator: purpose. What the brand stands for in the context of today's cultural complexity is what it represents and stands for

Instead of a fragmented and siloed culture where value is separated, a company's real-world conduct will be informed by purpose at every step of the way. This will lead to a unity of character and purpose. Because of this, brand trust seems to be dissolving or declining so strongly in the current post-factualism and post-truth age. This results in increased levels of brand trust. The return to integrity and brand trust can be achieved by direct accountability and behavior based on true beliefs.

By using all core processes and capabilities, the company would use one single symbolic denominator – whether it's through marketing, how the corporate processes are structured, what the employee culture looks like, and what customers care about and value in the company – in order to bring this meaning to life. Although it will be different for each of the company's fundamental capabilities, this holistic approach to management will result in more coherence, unity, and collaboration throughout the company's horizontal components. The company's internal culture will inevitably be aligned with the external culture (the cultural environment of the world outside), which would then effectively combine the two cultures into one. Today, as our society moves from division to unity, it is imperative for any corporation to perform such an enveloping act of cultural unification.

Rather than "striving for separation," corporations must now "embrace togetherness" and consider the value they provide from the point of view of the people who use them. They will be able to free themselves from the shackles of their everyday activities and processes, as well as their key performance indicators, thanks to this much-needed respite. Leaders of businesses and brands should look at their organizations as a living, breathing ecosystem of value creation rather than as a machine where all cogs - employees – must function efficiently at the optimum speed to keep the company running smoothly. Because it measures the wrong things, machine thinking is a major hindrance to developing meaningful purpose and long-term brand and business growth. Having a clear sense of purpose isn't just about aligning your company's internal and external values. As a whole, it has a profound effect on how we think about organizations and how they are organized to maximize value in the lives of its stakeholders.

Rethinking how organizations are built, how they create value, and most crucially, how they act to their employees, customers, and the greater world outside is essential if you want to use purpose in business to its fullest potential. Brands and organizations have a direct impact on society, thus their executives must know what values they wish to impart to the world.

The lack of a clear vision, corporate hypocrisy, and a phony sense of purpose can't be hidden behind a veneer of purpose. It's more than just a gimmick that businesses can use to mask their terrible reputations; it's an essential part of their brand's DNA. Authentic purpose is derived from a person's ancestry, the strength of belief and convictions, moral compass, as well as his or her vision and honesty. Adding anything that isn't already there is not possible. Those you want to see and things you don't want to see are magnified by it.

Those things aren't part of what makes anything a thing or determines how much something is worth to us. It's built in. This is the way we do business, the way we generate value, the way we spread ideas, and the way we get around in the world. Purpose is the primary channel through which we shape our thoughts, create stories, build our identities, and relate to one another and ourselves. Brands and enterprises are outmoded in a world without meaning, which is why they exist in the first place.

HOW TO GET PURPOSE INTO YOUR BUSINESS

The purpose and values of your firm should be clearly defined. Customer service, integrity, courage, growth, profit, cost, product innovation, quality, people, partners, the environment, responsible supply chain, sustainability, the list goes on: Get specific! What values and behaviors will the organization, its leaders, and its employees be guided by as a result of these terms? CORE values are a select handful (say, 3-4). Others, like integrity, are what I like to call "Fundamental VALUES" (they don't actually differentiate your company from others but define a baseline of behavior you expect and are ready to make tough decisions on). Prioritize your company's core values once you've established them. What are the most important and least important values? When the going gets tough, what are the essential values in your life? In making decisions, are there any guiding principles that the organization prefers to adhere to, and if so, in what order?

It's possible that an organization might state something like, "We want to expand revenue, but that cannot come at the expense of progress on our environmental goals; likewise, the progress on our environmental goals cannot stop our growth or the organization would cease to exist." Is honesty or integrity a value that cannot be compromised? If this is the case, then the organization's leaders must be brave enough to make the difficult decisions necessary to remain committed to the organization's Foundational Values. If not, its CULTURAL base begins to disintegrate, and its true SOUL is at risk. When the highest-ranking members of an organization's leadership team display a clear, consistent, and genuine commitment to the firm's mission and values, the company will thrive and prosper.

There should be a clear understanding of the role each member of the team plays in achieving the overall goal. Every profession and every department has a North Star that serves as a guidepost to your ultimate goal. Every day, in every interaction, and with every initiative, everyone should work to attain their goal. Policies, procedures, and processes should be designed to help you achieve your goals. What is your place in relation to the universe? Identify where you're out of whack. Your business should be geared toward assisting your team in achieving your mission. Emotions can and should play a role in the pursuit of a goal. The path to earning customers' hearts and minds is by winning the hearts and minds of your staff. In order to become a permanent part of your company, you must provide ongoing care and nourishment. Leaders need to convey tales about how they are making a positive impact on customers in order to keep their purpose alive. The new business narrative revolves around the concept of purpose. You'll be able to do more and establish yourself as a leader others want to follow. People are motivated by the desire to earn a profit. They, too, want to make a positive impact on the world. Your Noble Purpose gives you the ability to do both.

MISTAKES ORGANIZATIONS MAKE USING PURPOSE

To be successful, a company must have a clear and compelling mission. Many people aren't sure where to begin when it comes to finding their purpose. We've compiled a list of the most common blunders people make.

A nebulous goal: As a mission statement, "We're making a difference." You must have a clear goal in mind. In what ways do you make a difference? How do your customers feel as a result of working with you? What are the implications for each and every position in your company? Working with a purpose can be demonstrated in a variety of ways.

Associating philanthropy with a person's mission: The importance of social responsibility cannot be overstated, yet it is not an organizational goal. In the end, you don't get anything in return for what you're doing. Focus on the triple bottom line and be a decent or excellent corporate citizen. However, your goal is not on the opposite side of the bargain for financial gain. Your commercial model must be centered on your primary goal. Customers must be able to see value in the items you sell. You should be compensated monetarily if you are fulfilling your mission and providing value to your consumers. Making a project of your purpose: To begin developing a company culture centered on a mission, you will need to assemble a team. Purpose, on the other hand, is not a one-shot deal. In the long run, this is a way of thinking and acting that will endure long after your current workforce has left.

CHAPTER 10

AN IDEAL/GREAT WORKING ENVIRONMENT IS AN ESSENTIAL ELEMENT OF A COMPANY'S SOUL

When people envision their ideal workplace, they frequently envision one that offers opulent rewards, costly celebrations, and a bevy of other appealing amenities. A great workplace is more than just perks and advantages; it is a place where people are happy to come to work every day. Indeed, a great workplace is about the trust that employees have in their bosses, the sense of personal accomplishment that comes from their work, and how much they enjoy their coworkers' company. Although trust, pride, and camaraderie are considerably more difficult to maintain than a wonderful set of perks, they can all be achieved by any organization willing to put in the effort. The distinction between a decent company and a great one is whether or not it is a terrific place to work. Workplace satisfaction and organizational performance are directly linked to a company's cultural climate.

The workplace environment influences workers' motivation, job satisfaction, and team morale. In a favorable work atmosphere, employees are more likely to show up on time every day. Employer-employee interactions, the company's facilities, the company culture, and prospects for advancement are just a few examples of the workplace environment. In order to create a positive work atmosphere, employers must be deliberate. A company's reputation is built, and employee turnover is reduced in an environment like this. Employee productivity soars when they have a sense of purpose and fulfillment in their work. When you continuously follow the advice mentioned above, you will be able to cultivate a positive work atmosphere.

THINGS THAT MAKE UP AN IDEAL WORK ENVIRONMENT

A positive work environment is essential for attracting and retaining top talent, both in terms of new hires and long-term employees. Keeping your staff happy and motivated at work is essential if you want to keep them around for the long term. Remember that the ideal work environment may change from generation to generation; therefore, being able to adapt is essential for success. Remember that perks are no longer a reward; they're a requirement in the modern workplace. In addition to showing your employees that you care about their well-being outside of work, providing a competitive benefits package to new hires can influence whether or not they choose to join your company. Health insurance, 401(k) plan, and match, commute reimbursements, and subsidized cell phone plans are included in this.

Employees should do everything the same way they do everything else. As a company, we should live our principles both inside and outside of the company. For it, one must hold oneself and others constantly accountable. People who aren't actually living up to the company's values ought to be fired. Decisiveness should be highly regarded in the workplace. At all levels, people should be able to make their own decisions. Honor should be given to those who take prudent risks and make wise decisions in the face of uncertainty. When making long-term decisions, the company should focus on fixing the core causes rather than just the symptoms.

In order for an organization to thrive, its employees must place a high value on openness — openness to new ideas, new technologies, new ways of working, and so on. In my line of business, I enjoy dealing with people who want to learn more about the world around them. It would be a dream come true to work for a company where employees are encouraged to try out new ideas, put them to the test, welcome diverse viewpoints, and take risks.

Most full-time workers spend more than a third of their lives working. That equates to more than 90,000 hours of work. Therefore, the importance of having a good work-life balance is understandable when it comes to employee concerns. Take into account your employees' personal lives as well as their work lives if you want to attract new personnel or keep your current workforce pleased. For example, one of your employees may be a single parent who must be home in time to meet their child's school bus or commuting an hour or more every week, which is taking a toll on their family life. Flexible working arrangements, such as allowing employees to work from home, can boost employee morale and make your company more appealing to prospective employees. Employees should be taught and motivated to maintain a healthy work-life balance in an ideal workplace. To secure a promotion or raise, employees may be willing to put in extra hours each day of the week. It's up to management and supervisors to educate their staff about the positive effects of a work-life balance. Some employees are aware of the significance of striking a healthy work-life balance. Because of this, people prefer to work for organizations that allow them to take their yearly leave and vacation days on a more regular basis. Making it easier for employees to strike a work-life balance increases their sense of purpose at work. For example, they have time for their families, hobbies, and spiritual interests, among other things.

Recognizing the efforts of employees to enhance their performance can help employers build a healthy work environment. Employers do everything they can to meet their deadlines. Unpaid overtime may be required by some workers concerned about meeting deadlines and completing their projects on time. It inspires employees to accomplish more in the future if they are rewarded for their efforts. Employees, on the other hand, start making excuses for bad performance if their managers don't reward their efforts. There are many ways to recognize hard work, and money isn't the only one. In some cases, a verbal acknowledgment from the manager or supervisor suffices. Recognizing team accomplishments is critical, but so is emphasizing the contributions of each individual. Recognize and reward your staff for their contributions when you attain significant goals. The success of your organization is a team effort. Therefore, have a plan in place to recognize and reward employees.

Instead of focusing on effort, we should be aiming for excellence, real influence, and outcomes. A place where people support one another, encourage one another, and take tremendous pride in the accomplishments of one another is a terrific place to work. It's important that your employment becomes a source of personal fulfillment and that you're given the freedom to pursue your dreams. A large severance package and the option to find a new job should be made available to employees who no longer aspire to be among the best in their industry.

You don't expect to be performing the same low-level grunt work for your whole career when you start. It is a sign of your concern for your employees' professional growth and achievement that you provide them with opportunities for advancement. It's a win-win situation for employers and employees when they know that their superiors are invested in their success and growth. Look into professional development classes that your employees can take to learn new skills that they can utilize to grow their careers and your firm.

Training and development programs are a must-have in the finest workplaces. Employees will feel appreciated and rewarded if their employers are willing to spend time and money on training. When they can put what they've learned into practice, their motivation and productivity will rise. It is your obligation as an employer to ensure that your employees are prepared for the changes taking place in your field. The state of technology, for example, is constantly changing. Providing personnel with training in the usage of cutting-edge technology is a smart investment. In addition to hard skills, the curriculum should cover soft skills that can help employees better engage with each other and the rest of the company. Training employees in interpersonal skills, team building, dispute resolution, and effective communication will improve their interactions. Employees are more satisfied and productive when they have positive working relationships.

Employees place great importance on being recognized for their hard work and achievements. Most employees want to know that the effort they've put in during the course of a hard workday is appreciated, especially if they've gone above and beyond. Incentive schemes motivate current employees to achieve higher performance levels while also attracting new hires. Employees who go above and beyond could be rewarded with points exchanged for cash or other prizes.

Make sure you're open and honest with your employees about everything you're doing. Employees often complain that they aren't getting enough feedback or that the input they are getting isn't useful. Make it plain to your employees that they may come to you with questions if they are unsure about their expectations, and encourage them to do so. Annual reviews of employee performance are a typical occurrence. Both you and your employee may forget a great deal of what happened this year. You and your employee could benefit from a weekly one-on-one meeting or quarterly reviews, which will provide you and your employee more time to connect and get feedback.

Having a company that shares the same values as its employees might help keep employees motivated to put in long hours. When you run a firm, it's your responsibility to help your employees realize how their work contributes to the company's objective and provide them a reason to come to work every day besides their income. Employees are more likely to go the additional mile if their interests are aligned with your company's.

Employers frequently demand loyalty from their employees, but they don't always provide it to them in return. Although you can't guarantee that your employees will never have to deal with difficult situations at work, they should feel that their boss is there for them when they do. When employees are irritated or worried, they need someone to turn to for help, and providing that support builds loyalty. For employees to fully support the company's objective, executives need to be transparent about their own behavior and demonstrate that they hold themselves to a high standard of excellence. It's one of the characteristics of a successful manager. Exceptional leaders preach what they do, but they also take a stand on issues that affect the world around them with conviction. Leadership in their own firm should be devoted to increasing employee involvement, responding to employee issues, and promoting healthy company culture.

There is no such thing as a perfect organization. It is possible to develop a company culture that is aligned with the firm's values and goals by acknowledging shortcomings and having a clear understanding of employee involvement. For example, workplaces might use employee feedback to find out what makes a great workplace and what areas need to be improved. Talented employees are generally drawn to a company with a reputation for openness and honesty rather than a culture of secrecy and stagnation.

Communication is of the utmost importance. If you don't live up to the expectations of your employees, they will not be able to trust your leadership. When a supervisor doesn't set an example, it's common to see chaos in the workplace. To avoid the formation of undesirable habits, it is imperative that any guidelines, rules, and expectations are communicated immediately. An open and transparent line of communication between the workplace and the people in charge is also essential. Building trusting connections with employees is a result of listening to their concerns and addressing them. Employees have a right to a voice, and employers have an obligation to give them one. If employers don't act, employees will cease engaging in talks if they don't feel their thoughts and contributions are valued.

Having two-way communication in an organization guarantees that all stakeholders are on the same page regarding the company's goals. Sadly, many managers prefer to provide directions to their staff rather than collaborate with them. Approaching the problem in this way will yield the best results for the company, as it will explore all suggestions that could improve its performance. Since employees are more familiar with the systems and standards in place, they are better positioned to maximize productivity than management.

Successful companies do a lot of things correctly, but it's not always about what they do but rather how they do it. As a result, great workplaces are shifting their focus from maximizing the output of their people to ensuring the needs of their employees are addressed. There is a direct correlation between employee-focused actions and greater corporate outcomes. Firms may get right to the core of the matter by using employee survey data and discover where they're falling short. Using survey data to guide your company's growth is a win-win situation for both your employees and your business.

To succeed, one must be innovative. Every successful business relies on new ideas to keep things fresh. When a business is always innovating, it can remain competitive and take pleasure in its work. Employees are also motivated to produce their best work and contribute to the company's success through innovation. Assure employees that managers and even higher-ups will accept their ideas since they feel safe doing so. There is a good chance your employees are the ones who can help you find a solution to a problem you've been having.

Workplaces can be judged in many other ways, but a great place to work motivates employees and allows them to make use of their unique skills. Worker motivation is driven more by their work, rather than by the people they work for or with. They do their jobs for motives that go beyond the norm. Aim for consistent excellence in their work through fostering growth in their abilities and knowledge. Nowadays, a wonderful place to work is defined by today's workforce in this manner.

CHAPTER II

WHEN DOES A COMPANY REALLY FITS YOU – IT'S MUCH MORE THAN SALARY AND STATUS

Culture is difficult to analyze from the outside because it is implicit, and the comments about the company's culture may not mirror reality. However, I am confident that we will find a terrific place to work and join a culture that is a good fit for us. But, how? If you're a work idealist, how do you find an ideal workplace? You know, the kind of workplace where you get to experience the kind of love that so many people crave?

Finding a company that works well for you may be broken down into a few simple steps. Getting to know each other is the most important step. Stop acting like a stereotypical job seeker and start making new friends instead. Having dinner at a friend's house is a great method to meet intriguing, exceptional individuals in a non-intrusive way. People who want to make a difference in their careers, like you, enjoy talking about their personal lives. Make eye contact and shake hands with other individuals. Secondly, go to places where people who are mindful congregate. Avoid attending boring conferences and meetings as you execute the first guideline. Attending a Sarbanes-Oxley-related conference is not a good idea if you're looking for a job in accounting at a progressive company. Instead, go to exciting conferences and meetings on issues that excite you or where you sense "your tribe" of enthusiasts or like-minded/like-hearted people would congregate, rather than going to a boring lecture hall.

Make a list of all the things you want and need to succeed. What are the most important things to you? The following are categorical no-nos. No, I don't want to work at a place where I'm always being pushed. In a setting where you can interact with a wide range of people? Where will you be expected to make decisions and accept responsibility for your actions? Are you looking for a place where you may work-life balance is prioritized? Are you looking for a place with clear guidelines and expectations? The answers to these kinds of questions would be compared to my impressions about the company before I decided on a new position. I'd only agree to work on a project if we were a good fit.

To learn about the company's culture, go undercover. In order to get the full picture of a company's culture, you may need to seek outside of the company's blog and social media accounts. Your network can help you get a sense of the company's culture. Ask around to see if anyone you know has any connections to the company and can put you in touch with the appropriate individuals. Make an appointment to speak with them and inquire about their way of life. Find employees on professional networks like LinkedIn and send them a quick note asking if they'd be willing to take an informal phone conversation if you don't know anyone who does. Their response could be the first sign of openness and support if you're looking for that kind of quality. Internships at the company might also be an option for incoming graduates who want a first-hand look at the workplace.

You need to decide whether an organization is worth your time and effort after comparing the factors you desire with the information you acquired from calling other people or interning. Before submitting your application to these companies, I recommend making this decision so that you may focus your efforts on them. If you're torn between several offers and can't make a decision based on your assessment, I strongly advise that you follow your instincts. In the end, if you put in the effort and contacted people to learn more about the culture, you won't regret your decision. Listening to your gut while making a decision will help you make the most important decision of your life: the one that relies on your gut instinct.

Investing time in researching companies is essential. Even if you think you're accomplishing something by sending out a large number of resumes, you're squandering your time and energy. Even in a weak employment market, pursuing possibilities at a company that doesn't match your talents, credentials, and aspirations is a waste of time. It's not going to work out for you or the company in the long run.

Check out online reviews of the business you're considering doing business with. Before applying for a job, it's a good idea to check out company evaluations to get a better sense of the workplace culture, leadership, income, and more. Take a look at a company's total rating when reading company reviews. Compare the company's rating to its competitors and see if it is better or worse. For wages, benefits, and other important information, peruse employee ratings. Gather information from workers about their preferences and what they think could improve things. You should pay attention to what is mentioned about the workplace and other aspects of the company's culture and leadership. When assessing the profiles of potential employers, keep an eye out for any job opportunities or roles that have been suggested for you. You may discover new avenues to explore. See if any negative reviews have recurring themes that might point to a terrible employer. Be skeptical of what you read because every company has dissatisfied workers.

Keep an Eye on the Interview as a Whole: What's the Process? Going on an interview gives you the best opportunity to get a feel for the working environment and meet possible colleagues. Consider how the company conducts the entire interview process. Whether or not your contact at the company divulges the names of the people you'll be meeting with ahead of time is up to you. Do you get asked the same questions over and over again in each interview? Failure to work together is an obvious red flag during this process. It's possible that interviewers are just trying to fill time and don't have a clear idea of what they're looking for when they approach you. There is a possibility that the interviewers didn't plan ahead to ensure that they were assessing you on a variety of different aspects rather than repeating the same questions over and over. Regardless, it appears that the organization may not have a handle on defining your job and expectations. Would you feel at ease when working in a workplace that was riddled with confusion, sloppy work practices, and an unwillingness to hire the best individuals? That's a shocker!

Red signs should not be ignored! Regardless of the needs of the individual, there are a few warning signs that should never be ignored. A company's public image can indicate what they tolerate behind closed doors. Employees will be unhappy, and their careers will be stalled if they work in such an environment. Stay away from it. A terrible reputation as a place to work is exacerbated by elements such as dysfunctional teams and poor leadership, which job seekers frequently mention as reasons to avoid a company. It's for a good reason. Some issues, such as poor management, a hostile workplace, significant employee turnover, or a lack of work-life harmony, just cannot be remedied. The consequences are dire if you choose to ignore them. With a better economy and more powerful job seekers than eight years ago, company reputation is increasingly important. It's up to you to define exactly what it is and where it comes from.

KEEP THE SOUL AS YOU GROW!

While technology, customers, and society are continually evolving, one thing remains constant: companies must step up and have a purpose if they are to succeed in the future. That they have a soul and are thoughtful is essential. Commitment to organizational values must emanate from the top down, and it must start with the CEO! They must embody the principles that they want their firm to stand for and demonstrate consistency to those beliefs, even when the decisions they face are difficult to make. As long as employees can see the actions and decisions of the company's top leaders being consistent with its stated principles, they will begin to believe in the company's leadership. Leaders who do not "live the words," especially when things get tough or take unusual fortitude, are the fastest way to undermine the company's cultural base. When it comes to values, they can't just be stamped on a sticker or placed in a strategy as an endeavor that isn't followed through on.

Learn to track and communicate the progress of your company's values-based goals. What are the few important measurements that will tell you whether or not the company's values-driven goals are being met or exceeded? Then, be open and honest about the results of those measurements with the rest of your company. If no progress is being achieved, ask your teams what they believe needs to be done differently or what they believe is required to make better progress. Customers, investors, and consumers want to hear about this, but make sure it's real!

Consider tying compensation and performance to the company's most important values and metrics. Encourage team members to act following the company's values in their individual jobs, and at the levels of decision-making they hold within the organization. Increases in authority and the ability to make decisions are often accompanied by increased responsibility for achieving values-driven goals. Staff must recognize that company values are more than just words said by management if you want to keep the best people on board.

Cultivating a positive business culture has numerous advantages, including a competitive advantage. To put it another way, if you put your employees first, you're more likely to make money. Employees are less likely to burn out and are more likely to be productive. When customers and the general public see your company's distinct identity, it will help you stand out from the pack. Take a step back before installing a keg of beer next to the water cooler or setting up a yoga class every week in the main conference room. The foundation of a strong business culture is a thorough evaluation of a firm's basic beliefs and implementing those values from the top down through open communication, inclusivity, and consistency. When it comes to creating a positive corporate culture, it all begins with professionalism, appreciation, consistency, and trust between management and employees.

When it comes to hiring, it is also crucial to ensure that prospects fit in with the company's existing culture. Some employees may generate figures and profits, but negative culture fit can quickly spread throughout a team and firm. Unless senior leaders and managers take these critical steps to preserve the company's culture, no amount of compensation can save the business. You don't have to just emulate tech companies or lean startups, but rather show your devotion to your company's unique principles by acting in accordance with them. Your new keg may as well be delivering warm, stale beer without a real effort to improve the culture of your firm.

REFERENCES

Agle, B.R.R., Caldwell, C.B.B. 1999. Understanding research on values in business: A level Of analysis framework. Business and Society, 38(3), pp.326–387.

Asgary, N., Mitschow, M. 2002. Toward a Model for International Business Ethics. Journal Of Business Ethics, 36(3), pp.239–246.

ANSOFF, H. I., Corporate Structure: Present and Future (Working Paper, European Institute for Advanced Studies in Management, Brussels, 1974).

BUCHELE, R, B., Business Policy in Growing Firms (Chandler, 1967).

Collins, J.C., Porras, J.I., 1994, Built to Last: Successful Habits of Visionary Companies, Harper Collins Publishers: New York, NY, USA.

DE George, T.R. 1993. Competing with integrity in international business. New York. Oxford University Press. In Williams, S. L. 2011. Engaging values in international business practice. Business Horizons, 54(4), pp.315–324.

Donaldson, T. 1996. Values in tension: Ethics away from home. Harvard Business Review, 74(5), pp.48-62.

Forman, J., Argenti, P.A. 2005. How corporate communication influences strategy Implementation, reputation and the corporate brand: an exploratory qualitative study. Corporate Reputation Review, 8(3), pp. 245-264.

Groscurth, C. (March 6, 2014) Why Your Company Must Be Mission-Driven. Gallup.

HERZBERG, F., One More Time: How Do You Motivate Employees? Harvard Business Review (January-February 1968: 53-62).

IVANCEVICH, J. M., and DONNELLY, J. H., JR.. Relation of Organizational Structure To job Satisfaction, Anxiety-Stress, and Performance, Administrative Science Quarterly (1975: 272-280).

Kaptein, M. 2004. Business Codes of Multinational Firms: What Do They Say? Journal of Business Ethics, 50(1), pp.13–31.

Lencioni, P.M. 2002. Make your values mean something. Your corporate values statement May be doing more harm than good. Here's how to fix it. Harvard Business Review, 80(7), p.113.

Lipton, M., 1996, Demystifying the Development of an Organizational Vision, Sloan Management Review, 37(4), 83-92.

Mackay, H. 2017. Harvey Mackay: Values add value. Daily Herald. 3 May. Available: http://www.heraldextra.com/business/harvey-mackay-values-add-value/article_86023aba-

4875-53ca-85e9-f5c364dfcf1a.html. Viewed 16 May 2017.

Malbašić, I., Brčić, R. 2012. Organizational values in managerial communication. Management: journal of contemporary management issues, 17(2), pp.99–118.

Michailova, S., Minbaeva, D. B. 2012. Organizational values and knowledge sharing in Multinational corporations: The Danisco case. (Report). International Business Review, 21(1), p.59.

Mumford, M.D., Helton, W.B., Decker, B.P., Shane Connelly, M., VanDoorn, J. 2003. Values and Beliefs Related to Ethical Decisions. Teaching Business Ethics, 7(2), 139-170. Doi:10.1023/A:1022624222048.

Nahapiet, J., Ghoshal, S. 1998. Social capital, intellectual capital, and the organizational Advantage. Academy Of Management Review, 23(2), pp.242–266.

Paine, Lynn Sharp. "Managing for Organizational Integrity." Harvard Business Review, 1 March 1994, 106.

Stack, Jack, and Bo Burlingham. The Great Game of Business. Currency/Double Day, October 1994.

STEWART, R., The Reality of Management (Heinemann, 1963). The Reality of Organizations (Macmillan of London, 1970).

WILENSKY, H. L., Organizational Intelligence (Basic Books, 1967).

WORTHY, J. C, Organizational Structure and Employee Morale, American Socio-Logical Review (1950: 169-179).

AUTHOR BIO

Kurt Friedrich Gassner is an Austrian self-improvement author who empowers his readers to better navigate the intricacies of the unconscious mind. Through his lived experience and extensive knowledge of cutting-edge psychology, he helps people actualize their fullest potential. What started as writing for his peers in exchange for drawings at the age of 14 and later working as a professional copywriter, ultimately turned into becoming the Creative Director of multiple international agencies and the author of multiple self-help books.

However, writing isn't this entrepreneurial spirit's sole passion; Kurt has also been a serial founder (My Mind Guide and Trendguide Capital, to name a few) and Business Angel, garnering four decades' worth of expertise in the global advertising and brand consulting sectors. As a result, he has earned numerous awards in the areas of creative directing, direct marketing, and training and became a self-made millionaire. Utilizing his free time during the global lockdown, he even immersed himself in hypnotherapy and is now a Licensed Hypnotherapist, Yoga Instructor, and Meditation Teacher.

When he isn't running his businesses, consulting with leaders, or writing about the unconscious mind, you can find this globetrotter traveling around the world, golfing, biking in the Alps, attending the opera, or hiking. He is also the proud father of two successful children and happily married to his wonderful spouse of 37 years. Currently, he splits his time between Munich, Germany, and Kirchberg, Austria.

Throughout his life of innumerable toughs and crests, Kurt Friedrich Gassner has continued to live by the following motto unyieldingly: "Never stop! The best is yet to come…" And it is through his unwavering determination and perseverance that he has led a life of personal prosperity, learning countless invaluable lessons along the way. To him, a life lived without sharing one's acquired wisdom isn't a fulfilling one, so he creates books as a way of giving back and making this world a better place than when he first entered it. Some of his publications include The Power of Forgiveness, Lie or Die, Soul-Match, Can You Inherit a Poisoned Mind? And The Power of Poverty. When he was 30, he wrote a best-selling children's book that sold over one million copies and was used in kindergartens in German-speaking countries. Over a dozen other psychology-related books are presently in the works. Visit Kurt's official website to unleash your inner power and harness it for your greater good: gassner@my-mindguide.com

CONTACT US...

If you enjoyed this book and would like to read about other topics that have changed my life, please check out my new books on Amazon or my website: www.my-mindguide.com. Also, let's stay connected on social media. Please drop a line on Facebook or Instagram, and stay tuned for updates! You're welcome to share your thoughts with me directly as well: gassner@my-mindguide.com. In return, I'll send you a gorgeous infographic that you can cut out and frame. Please leave a review on Amazon, as this will help me to reach an even broader audience. Thank you so much for your time, insight, and undying hunger for knowledge!

I want to say thank you to all of my colleagues, clients, friends, and family members, who have all contributed to what I am now. I also want to say thank you to Gabriel Palacios, the king of hypnotherapy and a Swiss bestseller author who taught this old fox new tricks, letting me deep-dive into the mystery of hypnotherapy. I learned so much along the journey that I'm now a certified master-hypnosis coach and conversation coach myself! Furthermore, I want to say thank you to the fantastic teachers of SAMYANA/Bali who trained me to become a certified yoga and meditation teacher.

Last but not least, I give a special thanks to my master-teacher Eckhard Wunderle, who's close to a saint to me. He introduced me to the world of meditation and let me discover all the wonders it has to offer. I couldn't be more proud about having received my certification as a meditation teacher from directly from him at the Institut für Spirituelle Psychologie.

Peace, love, and happiness to all of you—till next time!

OTHER BOOKS BY THE AUTHOR

OTHER BOOKS BY THE AUTHOR

OTHER BOOKS BY THE AUTHOR

My-mindguide.com
THE BLISS OF STRUGGLE
WINNING STRATEGIES FOR DEMANDING TIMES
KURT GASSNER

My-mindguide.com
STARK DURCH „STRUGGLES"
DAS IDEALE MINDSET, UM KRISEN ZU MEISTERN
KURT GASSNER

LIE LYING & LIAR
A LIE HAS NO LEGS BUT IT HAS WINGS
KURT GASSNER

My-mindguide.com
LÜGE LÜGEN & LÜGNER
EINE LÜGE HAT KEINE BEINE, ABER SIE HAT FLÜGEL
KURT GASSNER

BORN
in the
COLD
Liebe und Aufmerksamkeit in der Wachstumsphase eines Kindes
KURT GASSNER

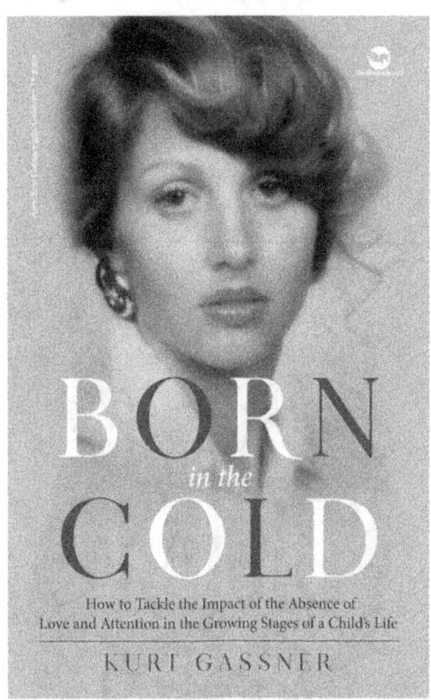

BORN
in the
COLD
How to Tackle the Impact of the Absence of
Love and Attention in the Growing Stages of a Child's Life
KURT GASSNER

SOPHIAS WUNDERWELT
10 ERZÄHLUNGEN
KURT GASSNER

SOPHIA'S WONDERWORLD
10 TALES
KURT GASSNER

BESTSELLING AUTHOR OF
The Art Of
FORGIVNESS
AMAZON #1 BESTSELLER
My-mindguide.com
A practical guide for
self healing and
overcome past traumas
The Art Of
FORGIVNESS
KURT GASSNER
My-mindguide.com
A practical guide for
self healing and
overcome past traumas
The Art Of
FORGIVNESS
KURT GASSNER